52 Motivational, Playful Columns on
Weight Loss, Habit Change,
and Other Acts of Faith

Striving for
Imprefection
per
(PERFECT crossed out)

By syndicated columnist
and THINspirational Speaker
Scott "Q" Marcus

Striving for Imperfection

Copywright 2006 by
Scott Marcus

ISBN: 1-59872-422-3

Printed in the United States of America

Cover design and layout by
Scott "Q" Marcus 707.442.6243
scottq@scottqmarcus.com

For additional copies of this book, or to hire
Scott "Q" Marcus for a speech or workshop, please
call 707.442.6243 or 866.SMARCUS.

You can also visit his web sites at
www.StrivingForImperfection.com
or www.ScottQMarcus.com

His first book,
The Shade of a Tree is the Very Best Shade There is:
135 Lessons for Your Children as they Move Up
is available at www.ShadeOfATree.com

More Praise for Scott's Writing

"I have been on the front lines of the weight
loss battle for the past 30 years. I attribute my
successes directly to your weekly columns."

~ Dick Wild
Parole Agent Supervisor & FBI Agent, Ret.

"When I find myself too serious, getting caught
up in daily life and forgetting to laugh. Scott's
writing style "recalibrates" me to a healthy
state of "lightening up." ...This is a medicine
man of the heart."

~ Jess Rose, Bilingual Mediator
Humboldt Mediation Services

"I look forward to the Tuesday edition of my
newspaper because that's the day of Scott's
column. His sharp wit and gentle humor
never fail to reach me at some level each time.
His column isn't just about (ugh!) dieting but
about how to live a truly healthy life."

~ Andrea Lawrence
Owner/Operator Midas Auto Service Center

"This is the first health column that I have read
all the way through. In one fell swoop I find
myself laughing out loud and seriously re-
assessing my health situation."

~Brian S. Millett
Writer/Youth Advocate

Dedication

This book might be my words, but it is the result of the faith, loyalty, and support of many. Should I list them all, this dedication might be as many pages as the text that follows, so I am forced to limit my gratitude to but a few.

Christine Sackey of the Humboldt Beacon in Fortuna, California was the first editor to give me monthly space in her paper. I am in your debt for providing ink to get me started.

Shortly thereafter, the Eureka Times Standard started publishing a weekly "To Your Health" section in its Tuesday edition. I called Charles Winkler, Managing Editor, and suggested that with my background in weight loss, and my ability to speak, I'd be a perfect match for his paper. After several (lost) emails and a few phone conversations, he took a risk "for a month."

Although this book covers my first 52 weeks, I continue to write for the Times Standard (and now several other newspapers); it's been about 18 months as the book goes to press. As for Charles, he's provided guidance in marketing and syndicating — an has always been supportive of my content. He's given me the names of people who might help. He's called others on my behalf. He's even taken me to lunch (a.k.a. "Salad, dressing on the side") — and paid for it!

I am honored by the continual support and am so pleased with our relationship. I owe you and I'm proud to call you a friend.

Of course, I there are my two sons, Daniel and Brandon, who support me in my writing, and most importantly, my loving wife, Mary Ann Testagrossa, the invisible muse of so many of the following pages. She has listened to each and every column (cringing when the subject matter came a bit "close to home") and always, always, always believed in me. I must have had a wonderful past life if my karma is so strong as to have her with me in this life. I love you. Thank you.

Finally, thank you to the countless people fighting their own demons who have found something of value in what I have to say and have called, written, emailed, come to my meetings, attended my presentations, or even stopped me in the grocery store or at the post office to share with me. I am proud of my ability to use words, yet your feedback honors me more than I can say.

To you, dear reader, thank you for picking up this book. I hope you enjoy and find some value and a little bit of humor in what I have to say. This book is most importantly, dedicated to you.

Treat yourself special - always. Enjoy.

Foreword

The alarm clock rattles, buzzes, and wretches. As I force myself to face my day, I am immediately overwhelmed with all I must complete, everything I must do — and immediately yank the blankets back over my head artfully, slamming the snooze button in one fluid motion.

There's always tomorrow; all things become possible in the new day. Today, I'll coast.

As a recovering perfectionist, I understand perfection is an impossible pursuit, yet for some unknowable reason I crave that title anyway. The hitch isn't my desire, it's my actions — or more accurately, lack thereof — caused by trying to be perfect instead of actually working to be better.

In past days, I thought I had to be "the perfect dieter:" avoiding EVERY snack, steering clear of ANY treats, and swearing off ALL nibbling. As life would have it, without thinking, I mindlessly munch a handful of nuts from my co-workers desk, a habit I've repeated countless times. Once I realize what I've just done, I am embarrassed and disappointed by my actions, as well as ashamed of my lack of willpower.

A decision is at hand. I mull my options, navigating the fierce storm raging within. I could consider this faux pas as human error, eat a little less tonight, congratulate myself for adjusting, and move closer to my goal.

Or, as a full member of Perfectionists United (known as "P.U."), chant our mantra (join me if you know the words), "As long as I blew it, I'll really blow it, and start again tomorrow." Soon therefore, an entire bowl of peanuts vanishes, as do extra brownies from the office party, and two bags of chips from the employee cabinet. I weigh more now than when the alarm blared.

What would have been a minor detour has become a full-stop road closure — because of my perfectionist objectives. When I try to break these bonds, they even slip cancer-like around my thoughts to undermine the cure: small consistent steps.

Fifty pounds is too much; five is not enough. Wait until you're ready to do it all. Running five miles is unrealistic; walking a block is useless. Sit down, relax; turn up the TV.

Black. White. Perfect. Awful. Success. Failure.

The world is nuanced with progress happening via minor movements; success gradually coalescing around the actions. One tentative step now, another thereafter — each a deliberate decision, each its own accomplishment.

This book is a collection of my first 52 columns, which are now syndicated in several newspapers. It started with an idea, than a phone call, than an email, than some typing. One day. One column. Now, you see the results.

It's not perfect; but the key to success — more ups than downs — was accomplished. I hope my thoughts give you some inspiration, a few laughs, and maybe even encouragement to move forward on your own journey — one step a time.

Don't even try to be perfect, just get better. Strive for imperfection. Treat yourself special.

Scott "Q" Marcus
April, 2006

Table of Contents

Striving for
Imperfecti~~on~~

per

PERFECT (crossed out)

The Anniversary

September 28, 1993: the worst day of my life.

Every facet of my being sobbed; my 11 year marriage was decaying, the muscles of my back never ceased their relentless spasm, and as I stood on the bathroom scale, "250 pounds" insulted me in unforgiving window.

I felt ancient. I guess it was therefore appropriate that we were "celebrating" my 39th birthday on that grey day.

Once the guests departed, I placed my birthday cake into its bright pink bakery box, closed the lid, and gingerly positioned it in the kitchen garbage atop wads of discarded wrapping paper. During the dark, lonely, places of the wee morning hours, I returned, kneeled, and – scooping with my hands - wolfed down the worn cake.

Obese since childhood, I was the fat kid last chosen, scoffed, insulted, accosted. "Husky" pants and XXL shirts were my trademarks. Self-loathing was nothing unusual. Nevertheless - that dark moment, on my knees, eating from the garbage - I plummeted to depths I had never known.

When one tires of walking into walls, it is time to open a door, no matter how painful the expected journey. So frightened, frustrated, and resentful - I reluctantly returned to my meetings after a decade-long absence. Promising myself I'd reach optimum weight by age 40, changing my life in 365 days seemed too swift. Weirdly, that same period seemed to stretch out unendingly into forever.

Night, day, hour, minute, I attempted to stay true to my vision. Emotions were analyzed, habits were changed, and patterns shattered. At times, 10 minutes of restraint felt like decades - culminating September 27, 1994 - 364 days from placing foot upon this path as the scale reflected a loss of 70 pounds: Goal Weight! A bright red LED flashing "179" was the only outward indicator of this momentous occasion. However, in my heart choirs of angels sang.

Weight loss does not make us better people; I am simply a thinner version of Me. Yet the process of change serves as an awakening of what can be accomplished with devotion, direction, and dedication. What powerful beings we mortals can be! Today - 11 years later - I am more proud of that accomplishment born of pain than any other decision I have made.

September 28, 1993: one of the best days of my life.

The Roots Of Change

Where reside the seeds of change?

What does Change do in its off-hours? Can one predict when its winds will fill our sails so we can tack our way to an island of greenery - or are we thrown suddenly a kilter, unwilling and unwitting victims of an unforeseen hurricane of transformation? Why do I plod on with my staid, ineffective course on Monday and throw all precedent into disarray come Tuesday? What lever caused me to at long last put on sneakers and walk off a few calories, or switch from whole to non-fat milk?

Experience tells me that change does not gently wash us anew with the soft coaxing light of gentle guidance; instead it is an unsympathetic taskmaster. I am human; I am prone to slack off. Only when the consequences of the status quo becomes overbearing will I buck up and face the unknown. Change, therefore, is the outcome of persistent fear, force, or pain, born of inactivity. It can be altogether a most unpleasant condition.

The paradox of transformation: If I remain as I am, indulging in ineffective patterns of comfort seeking (euphemism for "eating"), I magnify the crisis. Yet freedom from that routine's prison is stressful and tiring, generating the drive for comfort. I return from whence I started. The more I resist, the more I induce forces that haul me back. Said 18th century philosopher Voltaire, "God is a comedian playing to an audience that's afraid to laugh." I'm searching for humor here; maybe someone can explain the joke?

There is light. As with Hope emerging from Pandora's box, Change's companion is Vision. Stagnation, as relaxing as it might falsely appear, reveals no future, each day is merely a dulled replica of any previous period. What I was yesterday, I shall be tomorrow. This is not Life, merely the passage of time. Despite the tumult and travails of change, vision of a better place is what propels its engines.

For all the effort, if I stay mostly true to my course (or at least return quickly when I stray), there will be a quiet, reassuring, calm at journey's end. There, I will breathe deeply and enjoy the well-earned fruits of my efforts.

Gotta keep going.

A Child's Lesson

I am a child.

Grey hair, wrinkles, and an aging body are more apparent with each dawn. Lessons unexpected and sometimes self-inflicted impart knowledge unknown when a younger world. Yet, even now I remain astonished at rocket ships that touch comets; flung from millions of miles colliding in distances of blackness I cannot fathom. Head back straining to see, I stand mouth agape in awe of magnificent redwoods whose fingers touch the face of God. I cry and cheer for epic undertakings of movie-star heroes where good guys are virtuous and evil is always vanquished. "And they lived happily ever after…" is still a hope.

I remain so much the Child.

Dizzy days of rolling down grassy hills to lie upon my back and point out animals in the clouds exist no more, replaced with burdens of responsibility from morning alarm beyond day's last light. I yearn to play, scheduling it between doctor appointments and grocery shopping. I mourn the loss of simpler times when boo-boos were made "all better" with a kiss and a cookie. In today's runabout world, it is a six-pack, extra servings, or "comfort foods" to soothe my hurts. My adult knows I must change - but not today. For the young, there are countless tomorrows remaining for such undertakings; now is for extravagance.

The grown-up in me hears the ticking clock and insists there is no time for childish errors. My internal dialogue berates me: "Will you never learn? You're old enough to know better. You should be ashamed." Poison insults no teacher would ever utter, I hurl as stabbing weapons at myself, unforgiving, relentless, grinding, wounding. Alas, if guilt and shame were motivational, success would be mine today. Another thing I forget, so many lessons still to realize.

No matter how many years I traverse my path; I will trip up and sometimes fall. That is what children do. So much lies ahead and I desperately want to be "there" already. It is important to remember that guidance - not condemnation - illuminates the road. Loving praise for changes I have made, patience for what the future might bring, and support for what I am going through now will beckon a better way.

Curious, hurriedly, sometimes lost - and repeatedly stumbling - I am still very much a child needing to be reminded to stay the course.

To Feel That Good One More Day

My wife insists I stare. As a writer, I prefer to think I "observe." Therefore, I find myself at my local java house "observing" a young man as he prepares coffee. He attracts my attention due to his size. He is large. He is extremely large. I would wager my non-fat latte that he carries far north of 400 pounds.

Our eyes meet before I can avert my gaze. Whether it is the obesity from my own past, or that we really do communicate through the pupils - I cannot say. Yet at that instant, a tsunami of sadness slams into my soul.

A flood of yesterdays: Remembering when - embarrassed by my sheer mass - I wished no one would look at me. I hid while eating, not wanting others to know; a sulking overweight shadow of the dark places, all the while hauling shame and anger. Do others hide when they eat? Why must I apologize for my need to survive?

A consuming, heavy, dark, depression relentlessly pressed against my core - never resting, constantly gnawing, and stalking me through the nights. Whatever I did, wherever I went, I was its prisoner – unwilling or unable to change.

I am not so arrogant to assume that the coffee-sipping gentleman downtown feels what I felt or shares my experiences. I do not judge waist size, for I was sentenced too often.

The plain truth is in his eyes, all I saw was Me.

On cranky days, I still beg the Universe for a reprieve. "It's unfair I can't just eat what I want! I've been good. When do I get to relax?" There are nights when every ounce of strength I possess is applied to stay focused on my goal.

More than ten years have left since I reached "goal;" this pain surprises me, residing still so near the surface. I am not a better man due to my thinner physique. However, I am happier because another sunrise has passed to sunset and I held my old demons at bay one more day.

To hold that feeling in my heart a little longer, I shall continue.

Ode To My Pants

Mirror, mirror in my room
It's time to start my daily groom
In previous days, we've oft locked horns
Yet adorning myself 'twill be different this morn

I've followed my diet so sure and sound
My middle no longer as wide around
Trying clothes from the closet, I used to hate
With newfound pride, I do not hesitate

My favorite pants are top of the list
Compliments formerly heard have been sorely
missed
I yank the trousers around my waist
Anticipating grand results, I dress with haste

At first my feelings are somewhat confused
These pants are too tight; I am bemused
Inhaling deeply, my stomach sucks in
"What's this?" I wonder. "I'm not yet thin?"

I fuss, twist, stretch, and try to zip
Oh my goodness, did fabric rip?
Standing on tiptoes, trying to be taller
I suppose this should make my tummy smaller

I lift my stomach with one hand
The other is used to secure the band
I reach inside to find the tab
It will not go; still too much flab

I lie down on the bed upon my back
It seems I must try an alternate tack
I heave the snap into its place
Exhausted from effort, sweat covers my face

Rolling carefully and trying to rise
I begin to wonder about my size
It seems I have the slacks on now
Breathing would be nice; I'm not sure how

Stiff-legged I stand upon the floor
Success will be mine if I can reach the door
Like a movie monster, I lurch, not walk
My pants are so snug; I cannot talk

My stomach pains; I cannot bend
"Overstuffed sausage" described my rear end
The button in front is ready to burst
Better do something quickly or expect the worst

Falling against the closet, I remove my clothes
My stomach expands I can feel my toes
Relief comes quickly; blood starts flowing
These pants won't fit without loads of sewing

Sadly the truth I have to admit
If I wish to wear trousers when I sit
I'm exhausted, tired, and feeling blue
Maybe I'm not yet a 32

Weighing At The Doctor's Office

The visit to the doctor seemed unrelated to my weight, yet I am asked to stand on the scale. Why do doctors want everyone to weigh? Is there a per-pound commission? Do deliverymen have to stand on the scale before the receptionist will sign for the package? Questions left for another time.

My medical assistant did not realize she was dealing with a professional when she said she needed me to weigh. Precautions must be taken; delicate ego states are involved. My weight is not a number I take lightly (er, pun not intended).

Facing the scale, I inhale a deep calming breath. Why is it boldly lit and right smack dab in the center of the room? Some things are for the private places.

While she waits, I remove wallet, cell phone, money clip, change, keys, pen, watch, rings, belt, and finally, my glasses. If I wore contact lenses, I would have removed them also. I've got 13 pounds of love handles hugging my hips and I'm fretful about three ounces added by a writing implement; go figure.

This ritual holds no interest to her; she is showing etchings of frustration. "Mr. Marcus, please get on the scale."

"You want accuracy, don't you?" An unexpectedly high number could damage my fragile psyche, hurling me into a tailspin. How would my doctor feel if my cholesterol spiked 40 points due to a peanut butter binge induced by mistakenly thinking I gained eight pounds? Couldn't be good publicity for the medical profession, I'm sure.

Bending down and grunting, I untie a shoe. Trying to break the tension, I comment, "Pretty flexible for a guy my age, huh?"

Her eyes roll; she edgily checks her watch. "Can we hurry?"

"We?" I wonder. Seems like "Me." I choose not to point this out; soon she will know my weight and could blackmail "Us". Besides, I need focus. This is a delicate process to be executed with precision.

She is relieved as I remove my second shoe and start for the scale. Abruptly a horrifying realization dawns within me; I freeze.

She studies me, confused.

I explain. "While waiting I had a glass of water; that's eight ounces. I first need to use the rest room."

Samples

When did grocery warehouses become carnival midways, dotted with barkers hawking a cornucopia of tastes at every turn? Elderly ladies adorned in white, sterile, paper bonnets with green aprons cook at each aisle's end. Small microwave ovens ding and electric grills sizzle, providing the music for this legion of senior chefs to grill, bake, and fry as they entice shoppers to sample their wares. It is my responsibility to assist our elderly citizens in the economic pursuits of their golden years. As a moral person, I am compelled to taste.

I want to say "I'm just here for the free food," but that's rude. Instead, I feign interest and nod while I am informed of "today's special price" and great cooking tips - all the while devouring four miniature hot dogs, one cut-apart granola bar, and two diminutive burritos on toothpicks.

My preference is for the tables that are devoid of crowds, partially because being among a group increases the likelihood someone might ask that annoying question: "So, how's that diet working?" I hate that query, especially when delivered immediately before I pretend what I'm about to do won't affect my diet. Denial is difficult, even more so when a well-meaning friend is holding a mirror to your habit.

Also, the longer I think, the louder my pesky internal dialogue becomes. Conscience is a cruel master.

Skinny Scott: "Walk away. You'll feel proud; you'll lose a pound."

Chubby Scott: "A pound is overrated. Samples have no calories. They only count if they're on your plate."

SS: "If that were true, you wouldn't have put on weight from eating cold pizza while leaning over the sink all those years. Stop now. Lose the weight."

CS: "Don't worry; you will. Walking while eating burns off the calories."

Works for me. So, I embark upon the ritual of the strolling repast: One chicken nugget in half a napkin and a small paper cup of soup for the main course, two sporks of mashed potatoes, five tortilla chips with a spoonful of salsa, a tiny paper bowl of salad soaked in creamy dressing – and for dessert, one cookie, half a chocolate bar, and a baby spoon of ice cream. Nourishment complete, my diet a memory, I leave the store in time to get home for dinner.

Restaurants, Diets, and a Healthy Marriage

My wife and I have a regular lunch date each Friday. Although we would prefer warm, fresh, doughy, rich, chocolate chip muffins, reason usually overrides and we (begrudgingly) agree to follow our diet. Ah, the sacrifices we make to fight Father Time's clutches.

Weaving between segments of light conversation, I oh-so-casually inquire, "So, what are you going to order?"

Advanced observers of "dietorial" behavior will note that this query is not as innocent as it appears at first blush. If she replies - for example - "fish and chips," I act surprised and reply as such: "What a great idea! I was going to have salad but I'll have that instead." This alleviates me of the guilt of not eating healthy. Follow me please. As a supportive life-partner - in her best interest - I don't want my loving wife feeling self-conscious because she indulged in a fried food fest while I gently nibbled on lettuce leaves. Therefore I must consume an equal number of calories. For domestic tranquility, I sacrifice.

"I was thinking nachos…" she begins.

I can barely restrain my excitement; nachos are the mother lode! Three entire menus and two ice cream trucks have fewer combined calories than one order of nachos. I could inhale a deluxe burrito, beans, cheese and extra chips while still appearing to be on a crash diet compared to a serving of nachos. My wife is wonderful!

"… But I've been trying to lose five pounds," she continues.

My heart drops. Over the table, thoughts of guacamole and frosty Margaritas vanish in a puff.

An internal battle is joined. Inner Chubby Child wants her to order something gooey or greasy so I can have my "play foods" sans guilt. Adult Husband understands how difficult healthy choices can be and wants to be supportive.

"You're beautiful; you don't need to lose anything," slithers from my lips. Score one for child, husband bats zero.

She smiles, her deep brown eyes dancing. "Thank you. I'll still have the salad."

I sigh. Two salads: no sour cream, hold the taco shell, non-fat dressing - on the side. Green leafy rabbit food yet again. Happy happy joy joy.

While dejectedly picking at the greenery I try one last tactic. "Honey, with the calories we saved, what do you say we order dessert?"

The Morning Decision

I never really thought it would happen to me.

I had heard that it happened to everyone at some time. But, me? Nah. You gotta be kidding! I am exempt. Yet, my reflection shows salt and pepper hair and the deeply etched pathways of time branching from the corners of my eyes.

The future is at times so frightening close and real, I feel that if I lean forward, I will touch it. I understand we each must drive this long highway; it's just so unnerving when the largest part of it out the back window.

Upon rising, I challenge my reflection in the full-length bedroom mirror. Shirtless, analyzing my profile from the left, my eyes focus extensively on my soft, sagging stomach. I turn 180 degrees, as if this angle will drop six inches from my waist. No such luck. Gravity, too much time on a good couch, and a few too many beers have left their mark.

It has oh so definitely happened to Me.

I suck in my middle, stand taller, and throw back my shoulders. Babe Magnet has arrived, watch out ladies! Yeah, right. At this very moment, there's a supermodel in a $2000 bathing suit quitting her assignment on a warm tropical beach to jet to Eureka because I held in my midsection for 30 seconds. The male psyche is a fantasy-filled place.

I relax my muscles with a sigh. Even Ponce de Leon died, why fight? If I gotta go, I'd rather my last meal be fried than fresh. Consider the people on the Titanic who skipped dessert. What good did that do them?

Yet fifty-something has its moments. The gamesmanship of young relationships has been replaced with fine and loving friendships. The world disappears when my wife wraps me in her arms on a Sunday morning. Maybe best of all, I am appreciated - even by me. These days have a unique, refined, splendor worth savoring and sharing. They are definitely worth the effort.

I look back at the warmth and softness of my bed; who would fault me for climbing back in on this foggy, chilly morning? I glance again into the mirror, put on my shirt, lace up my walking shoes, strap on my iPod, and head into the dawn to exercise.

Life is good.

Denial, Deceptions, and Other Dietary Fads

I am starting a movement. Well, I'm not exactly sure if one "starts" a movement; they're probably more organic and start of their own volition. Nonetheless, I'm going to do my gosh-darn best to quash the ridiculousness of some of the dieting trends that have invaded society. It is my duty as a professional dieter. I have a voice; I must speak!

I was silent when the low fat movement hit its zenith several years ago. C'mon folks, not everything low fat is healthy. Some candies tout "no fat." Health food? I think not. Vodka is made from potatoes. Can we possibly imagine the absurdity of Mom coaxing her unwilling child with, "Drink your vegetables or you don't get dessert?"

Then came the seemingly unending low-carb epoch; a time in history where even beer promoted net grams. They didn't blatantly say "healthy," but at the height of that craze – when people were frying lard in butter and proclaiming it health food – "low carb" was translated into "keep eating; it's good for you." I almost protested then, but my mouth was too stuffed with bacon, steak, ham, and eggs to speak.

With that fad fading, we now find ourselves adrift in search of the next "eat-all-you-want-but-don't-change-a-thing-and-still-lose-eight-pounds-a-day" miracle diet, soon to be splashed on magazine covers in screaming red bold type. Be wary. The other night a commercial caught my attention because the announcer was talking about balance being the key to long-term health.

"A lighthouse of sanity appears through the fog," I think. Alas, my delicate dietary dinghy was depressingly dashed among the rocks of dopiness as images of sugar-laden, chocolate-covered, peanut butter marshmallow bars attached to descriptions of "nutritious, sensible, and healthful" flittered across my TV screen. I know I'm spending a lot of time perched on this soapbox but simply slapping a label of "healthy" on a product does not make it so. Painting my bicycle red and sticking a bell on the handlebars will not make it a fire engine.

I have kept my mouth shut too long (um, except for that late-night eating issue). It is time to rise up! And as soon as I finish my low-fat, high-fiber, all-natural, zero calorie, polyunsaturated, sodium free, no-carb, lactose-reduced, sugarless, cheese-flavored diet nutrition bar, I've got a good mind to write a letter.

Science Marches On

You could hear the nationwide cheer that erupted when the University of Colorado announced recently, "fat thighs might be beneficial to health." Really! Pour some extra creamer in your coffee and read on. I would not make this up; that would be cruel. We can neither slow aging nor cure the common cold, but by golly, we can trash-toss those tortuous thigh-toning machines! Say Hallelujah brother!

The study reports that we have healthier "peripheral fat" (limbs) and "unhealthy visceral fat (stomach)." According to a professor, "pay more attention to waistline fat rather than thigh fat". Oh sure, easy to for you to say; you probably look great in shorts. Oops. I digress.

Per the study, the "benefit of fat thighs" is that they were linked to better triglyceride scores. Not only has a new day dawned brightly for those of us mistakenly trying to firm, tone, and shape, but you are - at this very moment - reading the first time in history that the terms "fat thighs" and "benefits" were ever linked in one sentence. A truly historic day!

"Fat Thigh Benefits" (that expression will take some getting used to) are enhanced if one has a thinner upper body. Hmmm, thin top, heavy bottom. We're picturing as the future pinnacle of healthy body image those round-bottomed toys that don't fall over. Think Calista Flockhart above the waist and Kirstie Alley below.

Don't misunderstand; I'm not making fun. I have more than my share of unsightly leg and stomach "dimples" ("pot holes" is more accurate). I suck in my stomach so often I could replace our vacuum cleaner.

My concern is how this discovery could be misinterpreted. Instead of gyms packed with puffing, panting, people, "4T" specialists (Thick Thighs Tiny Tummies) might hang business shingles from every corner promising pencil size middles and overdeveloped limbs. Popeye could emerge as a national role model. What country would interact honestly with a nation who's prestige is represented by a cartoon character?

Yet, there could be advantages. Instead of trying to hide those jiggling, wobbly gelatinous, masses I call my legs, I imagine some poor skinny soul envying my hale and hearty limbs. "I wish I was healthy as you," he sighs.

"Just keep at it pal - and put some more butter on those mashed potatoes."

Zombies and Talking Food

Food talks to me.

I don't mean to say I have long in-depth, emotionally connected, heartfelt meetings with a head of cabbage. Yet, at night, on my way to bed, I hear voices calling to me from the kitchen. Crackers beckon me to find them in the pantry. Ice cream's siren call of my name floats across the dark room from the freezer.

"Scott," I hear the invitation, "Do you really want to sleep now? Wouldn't you rather have a quart of chocolate mint?"

"No," argues the cracker box. "Have something crunchy and salty - much better."

The disagreement continues. I stand transfixed, listening. (After all, I don't want to be rude.) Finally, in the interest of keeping all sides happy, I eat both... followed by cereal, cheese, and peanut butter.

I would weigh 50 pounds less if I'd just go to bed five minutes earlier each night.

One of the larger problems in weight loss is late night eating. Calories in – calories out is the bottom line (no pun intended). However, eating late tends to be less healthy as we consume more (because we're tired or bored), and then immediately lower our metabolism (by sleeping). Our sleep is less restful and morning brings a bloated belly and guilt, further lowering our resistance – and perpetrating the cycle.

Zombies we are not; suddenly driven to eat when the clock strikes the witching hour. It is the culmination of many habits of the dark that drive us to eat. We sit in our usual lazy boy, wear the same sweat clothes, and adjust our lighting in the same manner every night. Notice that even our snacks are same type usually.

It can take just adjusting ONE trigger to generate a new feeling, leading to different self-talk, generating positive results. For example, instead of waiting until bedtime to brush your teeth, try brushing after dinner. Or sit in a different part of the living room. Instead of watching TV, call a friend - or read.

Come the sun, the results will be higher self-esteem, a more restful sleep, and the beginnings of a smaller waistline.

Yes, it will feel odd not having your old habits joining you for the evening. But soon, these new habits will feel as comfortable as your pajamas.

Food Pushers and Other Acts of Sugar

I beam with pride at my image in the mirror; finally able to button my pants without having to lie on my back. The number for my waist size is smaller than my age for the first time in years. I am ready to strut my middle-aged stuff at our annual holiday party.

Sarah, the hostess, greets me with "air kisses" next to each cheek, gleefully exclaiming "Honey, let me look at you! You're just wasting a way! Here, have a teeny-weeny slice of pumpkin pie. Don't worry about how much work it took to bake it the way you love it. You're worth it (guilt-inducing dramatic sigh). You can start your diet again tomorrow." Maple syrup and a graham cracker crumb crust now possess her. She is channeling pure sugar.

Noticing my resistance, she adds in a baby voice, "Just one itty-bitty piece," punctuating the sentence by shoving a SUV-size dessert towards my face.

Moral dilemma: Why is it considered wrong to offer a cigarette to a reformed smoker while acceptable to force a plate of sugary, syrupy, sweets to someone losing weight? What kind of insensitive dolt would tell a reforming smoker, "Here, it's just one teeny-weeny cigarette. I rolled it just the way you like it."

"Food Pushers" are well meaning but unaware of the internal struggle we face while losing weight. They believe they are lightening our load by making it "OK" to eat.

To handle their pressure (while maintaining the relationship), recognize the INTENTION of the behavior and re-direct the pusher. Instead of "You're always trying to ruin my diet," and storming away in a huff, try, "Thank you for making this. However, it's important to me to stick with my plan; I'm so happy with the re-sults. Would you mind getting me some of that delicious coffee instead?"

The pusher is recognized for loving intent while given a new direction. It doesn't always succeed, but the key to dieting is to have it work more times than it doesn't.

In a pinch, you can feign food allergies: "I'm al-lergic to that food. If I eat it, I'll swell up." It is true when you think about it. Then, smile gently, wish them well, and slip away into the crowd.

When the Holidays are No More

If a therapist's couch were available, she would lie upon it and recap stories of childhood and chocolate. Instead, seeking solace, she bemoans the difficulty of dieting in December. "Parties. Candy. Cookies. Why not just give up and start again in January? Any advice?" I smell marshmallow chocolate Santas on her breath.

I validate the feelings. Although I have maintained my weight ten years, the struggle remains. "I understand."

As for the advice, she would not want me running her life. It can be a dark and scary place inside where I live. I understand her frustration. Yet, I have been asked. I push aside my cobwebs to impart whatever support I can provide.

I too used to "wait until the holidays were over." Then, my birthday… Then vacation… Back again to the holidays… Soon any day that ended in "Y" was a reason to delay losing weight. The perfect day was always over the next sunrise. I waited. I weighed. I weighted. Finally realizing future generations will still be overeating at holidays long after I'm a memory, I understood, "better figure out a way to work around the obstacles NOW." As my grandmother said, "Tomorrow never comes."

Reality is if my indulgences were limited just to holidays, I wouldn't have to lose 70 pounds.

Celebrations were the validation I used to reaffirm that "weight loss is too hard." Failure sat at the head of every holiday meal table as the unwelcome guest, "Give up – start again later."

That became the excuse for my black and white thinking, "as long as I'm 'off' program, might as well enjoy it!" What would have been three sugary cookies, a glass of eggnog and a shot of rum, become a tin of the first, a quart of the second, and a fifth of the third. Two pounds grows to five and expands to ten. I'm heavier and sadder than when the year began. Cycle moving backwards.

There is no Christmas dieting miracle. Strive to do well – don't even look for perfect. It is better to do "pretty good" right now and keep moving forward slowly, than to promise complete flawlessness next month. January is not as much of a rocky road (pun lightly intended) and you will be further along.

The Blessings of Obesity

"For my final column of 2004, I will write a motivational inventory of all the great things about dieting," I announced.

"Short list," came the reply.

It does appear anything BUT uplifting having to avoid favorite foods, be more active, and analyze your eating. So, work with me people, work with me. Experience maybe a lighter step in your travels.

Truth: That which causes the most pain – when faced - generates the most pleasure.

Before thinking I've imbibed a few too many Hot Toddies (using non-caloric sweetener instead of honey), I didn't always realize how "lucky" I was to have to drop so many pounds. I cursed my background, society, even the universe. A conspiracy of Skinny determined my weight. "Not my fault," I proclaimed, "I've tried EVERYTHING" (as if everything always works first time). Until I took emotional possession of my 44-inch waistline and faced the hurt of my part of my obesity - my life was rented, not owned. As it's said, "No pain, no gain." (Um, er, wording in that expression my not be completely accurate for weight loss – but you get the gist.) Upon acceptance that it was ME who would shoulder the work and make the changes, I was awarded the gift of Self.

Since then, embarrassment has morphed to empathy, drawing me close to many, enriching the fabric of my life. Backaches banished now provide a youngster's joy at touching my toes without a written plan. Shame blossomed to openness; I now share and accept. In meetings, I am connected to hundreds facing their demons. En masse we push forward, learning, growing, each inspiring another. We appreciate success, not fearing as much the slides, understanding that too is part of this process.

From that knowledge, I am thinner – and happier - because I like more about Me.

There are other paths to growth. However, I can do nothing about my own yesterdays, save use them as counsel for tomorrow. Today, I thank the Universe for my gifts, many of which I would not have seen if I had not had to first look within and face that battle.

For 2005: Peace - from within for everyone - for all from each of us.

Fitting Room War Story

Nothing brings out more anxiety in the "professional dieter" than trying on pants. I have come up with some mighty fine excuses to get over the trauma (if I do say so myself). Try this: "Clothing made in other countries fits differently; something about the translation of numbers from one language to another causes them to be too snug."

A mind that can twist reality into such a distorted path obviously has issues. I mean my head knows my waist is 34 inches; it's just that I fear overnight I ballooned to 107 and everyone has noticed but me.

Therefore, nervously, I cross the threshold of the fitting room. The white, plastic, dangling security tag on the trousers announces a deafening "ding-dong" that reverberates through the store drawing unwanted attention. I am convinced I hear a woman comment, "Poor misguided fool. Those will never fit. He's obviously a 38."

With consternation, I slide into the slacks. There were many days when passage to my waist was blocked at thigh level. Today will not be one of those bleak moments. Inhaling deeply, I prepare for the acid test. Sweaty fingers feverishly working the button, I raise my belly and reach to fasten it - in vain! Panic explodes!

"I have gained weight!" Gulping deeper, I lift so much of my stomach that my chest sticks out. I cannot see my waist; I must use touch to guide the fastener to its rightful target a second time. Again, the results are the same.

Vanquished and defeated, I remove the pants to inspect them. Hoping against hope that they were wrongly sized to 24, I find relief. The buttonhole was sewn shut, a nasty practical joke inviting heart attacks in those less observant.

I replace the slacks, inhale, slide the button into place, and release my stomach. I can breath – good sign. No embarrassing "riipppp" coming from my hindquarters when I sit. The pants have exceeded minimum standards.

While heading for the cashier, I go by the shirts and pause, deciding about whether to try one on. The wiser path would be to face that battle another day. Today, I shall savor the sweet taste of victory.

Honesty in Packaging

In the good ol' days, "one serving" of food equaled one container. A simpler time, I didn't seek counsel from nutrition labels and count out "14 medium sized chips" or use my orange plastic measuring cups to determine "two ounces, including sauce." Container size mattered not. A diminutive can of mushroom stems and pieces or a "bucket size" of peanut butter or ice cream all fell under the heading: "one serving." (Helpful diet tip: Any food packaged in a plastic bucket is probably not designed for quick weight loss.)

Nutrition Facts labels have forced adjustment from yesteryear's uncomplicated times. I peruse the sides of boxes, monitoring saturated fat, sugars, and sodium before loading my shopping cart. Grocery stores are classrooms; I am tested every week.

At times, I remain perplexed.

Muffin mix boasts two options: "Dry Mix" and "As Prepared." I've been known to devour a tube or two of cookie dough in my time. Yet consuming dry mix right from the box - what is the proper etiquette? Do I use a tablespoon or simply pour the powder in a bowl and scoop it with my hands? Why would the label even list that option? Please enlighten.

The champion of all confusing labels is awarded to microwave popcorn. Whoever determined these portions deserves to be boiled in the same hot oil used inside those unearthly bags.

Let's be honest, shall we? Popcorn's "official serving size" is "one bag" (previous comments about portions not withstanding). For argument's sake, I'll assume there are some who don't eat the whole thing, choosing to share a bag of salty, crunchy, goodness with family members - and not consume it voraciously by themselves while watching TV. I have not met these folks – but I attribute that to the fact that I tend not to travel as much among the Skinny.

That aside, the kicker is that the label states – I kid you not – serving size: "two tablespoons unpopped." Go ahead; pick up the box. You'll see. What's that about? Does ANYONE shred open one of those bags and scoop out two tablespoons?

"Honey, could you pour some hot oil in my mouth to pop these kernels? Don't forget the extra butter please."

By the way, don't even get me started on ingredients labeling.

A Tribute

Ruth Marcus lost 80 pounds at age 69.

Having fought the battle of weight since she was a teen, my mother knew more about fat grams and calories than nine nations of nutritionists. Indelibly imprinted in her gray matter was every food fact label on Earth. She could – and would - fill eight hours of a ten-hour road trip reciting from memory the fat and fiber content of countless foods – some I didn't even know existed. (The other two hours were reserved for finding restaurants.)

With the kind of grief that makes it difficult to breathe, I began the process of emptying her car's trunk after she died. I removed a self-made earthquake preparedness kit inhabiting a brown cardboard box. Neatly arranged were all the appropriate post-disaster supplies: batteries, bottled water, and canned food (of course). Buried under a brown tarp next to the butane lighter, was a plastic four-sided object. Slipping the item from its repository, I recognized it as a portable food scale for dedicated dieters when one is not near a kitchen.

A bittersweet smile found its way through my tears as I pictured the thought process that would have led her to include this particular article among the most important items one would need post-apocalypse. Did she foresee

California leveled by a 10.4 shaker; survivors huddled under tattered blankets among the collapsed ruins? As they warmed themselves by campfires - hoards of starving, grimy individuals scrounging for food - one lucky survivor discovers a package of crumbled, tired saltines among the remains of a mini-mart. My mother, always the helpful dieter, would whip out her portable scale announcing, "If you're worried about putting on a few pounds, I can measure out the correct portion size for you."

Last week was the anniversary of her leaving this world - a hole in my life still unfilled. Yet, I can picture her in the afterlife, even now watching over me with ever-smiling eyes. As angels serve cakes, wines, and heavenly treats, I see her politely raising her hand, smiling warmly, and replying, "No thank you. I'm watching my weight."

My sister, Cindy Kobler, and I founded a scholarship for aspiring writers in honor of Ruth Marcus, our mother. You can find out more from the Humboldt Area Foundation or simply mail a check referencing the above to Alexandra Reid, Donor Services Coordinator, Humboldt Area Foundation 373 Indianola Road Bayside, CA 95524 707.442.2993 or at www.hafoundation.org

Of Exercise Machines and Torture Devices

I hate exercise. It reminds me of junior high P.E. and smelly locker rooms. As a "husky" child - showering among testosterone-crazed adolescent jocks reserved a special place in Dante's lowest levels of the Inferno.

On cooler days, when gym clothes were not required, I "ran" (if walking punctuated by labored breathing can be called that) in brown corduroys, generating a "swish-swish" of fabric between my legs. Barely more than a whisper, the sound seemed to me a blaring announcement over the school loudspeaker, calling attention to the heft of my limbs. The threadbare patch of cloth between my thighs caused by continual rubbing was a scarlet letter of embarrassment – a reminder of my lack of prowess on the school track.

Therefore - I now carry "baggage" about exercise. To ease this pain, I refer to it as "activity" – a softer term. Call a horse a cow; it still won't milk. Ah, the twisted paths we weave.

Wearily, I awake to do my "activities" in the spare room. First, one must make sure the workout environment is pure - can't exercise if the room's askew. Dust on the windowsill? Breathing problems. Better clean it up. My workout promotes itself as "Eight Minutes." Proper room prep takes five times that. Any excuse in a storm.

I begrudgingly huff and trudge though 24 repetitions of lifting dumb bells (there's an irony in that name somewhere but I can't grab it), jogging in place, crunches, and a ghoulishly twisted floor posture medieval torturers would find curiously fascinating. The rhythmic drone of the announcer twists and turns my worn out bones until "cool down."

The term "cool down" should be associated with babbling creeks, light breezes, and lazy days. Stretching and contorting while ripping muscles from bones, all the while trying to touch my forehead to my calf is not "cool down". I am circulating a petition to change the name. Please sign it.

Finally, the best part: shutting off the tape. Health increased. Self esteem up. Body aches enhanced.

Yet, the most maddening detail is not the exercise, er, activity. It's the falsehood of losing weight for the effort. On the scale this morning - no weight loss! Nada! Zip! And I've been exercising religiously for two straight days!

No Resolutions This Year

Did you hear that? At precisely 12:01AM January 2, the giant clunking sound rumbling across this wide land was the consciousness of the population shifting from "how much can I eat" to "how can I lose weight?"

This communal retrofit (more accurately "retrofat") infiltrates every corner of society. During dark of night, grocery store displays transform from chocolate snowmen and cookie tins to low-fat crackers and high-fiber breads. Lines explode at gyms, driven to frenzy by dreams of six-pack abs. Diet centers burst at the seams (literally and figuratively). Reliable sources say even Santa was using his treadmill.

Last month dieters were alone, isolated from the countryside of high calorie goodies. With January's dawning, we are praised by the newly re-converted masses (and oh boy, there is some mass). A family reunion; we are showered by the returning with compliments about will power and waistlines. The sun is shining. The rain is gone.

Despite the fresh-faced enthusiasm of newfound aspirations, many fall victim to the well-intentioned "New Year's Resolution". Expecting unreasonable results previously unattainable the first 38 years they were attempted, these dedicated (now heavier) souls insist, "This time it'll be different. This time it'll work." Why the universe will mysteriously and suddenly change its rules to accommodate their healthy desires is left unexplained. Yet, undeterred, they pledge with resolute determination to run five miles a day, drink only water, and eat only carrots.

The only useful resolution is, "Rid oneself of unrealistic resolutions."

Small steps repeated regularly ALWAYS get superior results to large steps done intermittently. Translation: better to walk a block and do it than promise to run a mile but sleep in. Success is achieved more consistently by setting small goals that blend smoothly into everyday life, rather than by trying to uproot one's entire lifestyle into a new dimension. Small step. Repeat. Small step. Repeat. Consistency breeds success. Decades of old habits will not flee in 365 days. Drink just one more glass of water a day. Park at the far end of the lot – and walk. Lower the sugar content – don't sacrifice everything.

If lifestyle changes required are too involved, circa mid-January, that well-meaning resolution will be relegated to the attic among the holiday decorations gathering dust until next year.

In Other News...

I have a suggestion for the front-page headline:

**MARCUS WEARS BELT ONE NOTCH
TIGHTER - WITHOUT SUFFOCATING.**

I am not unsympathetic to the responsibilities of the editor; I realize there is other news in our little burg nestled on the coast. But - in my world – this headline is a 500-point bold font, above-the-fold, screamer! MY BELT HAS ONE LESS HOLE TO CONQUER! The public needs to know this. Didn't some philosopher say something akin to, "One man's success enhances everyone?" Therefore isn't it morally wrong to hold this information from our county?

OK, I'll admit it's happened before. But on those occasions, I yanked, pulled, and tugged the leather around my midsection to make it stretch; holding in my stomach, daring not to exhale or sit. This time, it's different! I pulled the belt to fasten it and it went further – all by itself!

Amazed, I needed confirmation in the mirror. Maybe, while I slept, some pod-like aliens substituted for the real me a skinnier version of their human captive. Grey hair, oversized ears, goatee. Still me. Wow!

I stare intently at my profile in the reflection, pushing in the couple inches around my navel for confirmation. "Houston, we have belt-fastening." I move closer to analyze the image. "By golly, that's definitely my stomach under that taut belt. If this ain't newsworthy, nothing is!"

Since everyone must know, I slide this information into seemingly unrelated conversations.

"Ten dollars," says the store clerk, "Cash or credit card?"

"Credit card," I reply, swaggering and reaching into my back pocket, accentuating my stud-like figure. "You know," I mention casually, "It's much easier to get my wallet now that my belt is tighter." I fix her with a John Wayne stance. She looks at me as if I'm Don Knotts.

I admit I'm proud of this. If I can focus on these little changes in my program, I'll do much better than thinking about how far I have to go. My attitude does benefit from broadcasting my success. But on the other hand, the first amendment was founded on the public's right to know. I am merely doing my duty as a patriot, keeping the constitution strong.

When I lose 10 pounds, I'm calling 60 Minutes.

Confessions in Aisle Four

I wish not to burst your bubble but - truth be known - I don't just eat "healthy stuff." I have feverishly consumed an extra large order of fries once or twice. (There, I've admitted it. Now, can begin the healing process.)

Therefore, no one need apologize to me for his or her eating transgressions. While on the subject – with all due respect – please do not inspect my grocery cart for only low fat products. Being mortal, I will fail and get cranky. Judge me not, lest ye be disappointed.

With that background, understand the apprehension that permeates me when I spy a woman bee-lining toward me at the supermarket. I have a sixth sense about this; she is seeking absolution for slipping on her diet. Unconcerned that I am not adorned in a minister's collar she confesses, "I want to return to meetings." She proceeds without introduction, "I've just been so busy. Don't give up on me. I'll be back." I nod. She giggles nervously and disappears behind the frozen foods, leaving me wondering whom she was. My path in life is populated with people I don't remember telling me intimate details about what they eat.

Next is Frank, hefting a generous waistline. He approaches from behind the canned vegetables and inspects my grocery cart with either a scrutinizing – or hungry – eye. Launching a pre-emptive excuse, he begins, "I lost these 30 pounds last year doing the low-carb thing." He satisfactorily pats his expanse with a jovial Santa-like quality.

"Worked great," he adds, waiting for acknowledgment.

I try not to stare at his stomach. My definition of "worked great" would be that he'd have a smaller waist. Oh goodness, my internal voices can sometimes be catty!

"Worked so well, I'm doing it again," he concludes.

A wicked thought scampers across my mind, "if the diet was so effective, why does he have to do it again?" Forgive me one more time; seems I can't control the voices in my head.

So, together let us take a pledge. Raise your hand. (Put down the chocolate.) Repeat with me: "I will not watch what others eat nor buy."

The pressure of hiding my food is enough to make me eat.

Dieter's Dictionary

Every group has its own language, including dieters. In the interest of better communication with the thin, I have compiled several terms and expressions used by those of us working to achieve such status so that we may all speak the same language.

BATHROOM:

(1) a.k.a. "weight reduction cubicle"; private location to relieve oneself of extra poundage before weigh-in.

(2) Location of *SCALE* where dieters repeatedly pay homage, sometimes before and after visiting *BATHROOM.*

CALORIES:

Invisible units with enormous power to influence size - and therefore mood - of dieters *(also CARBS and FAT GRAMS)* Calories have unique mathematical ability to be undercounted no matter how diligent a dieter strives for accuracy.

DIET:

Four-letter word derived from "die" *(ironic because being on a DIET can generate thought "I'd rather DIE than eat like this another day.")*

EMOTIONAL EATING:

Is there any other kind?

EXERCISE:
  Dreaded - often avoided - activities involving sweating, panting and bouts of hyperbole. Example: "I ran a mile." Actual: "I walked to the mailbox."

FAT:
  (adjective) The "F-word" *(not to be used in polite company)* to be replaced with "full-figured" or "big boned"

  (noun) apparently intelligent form of cellular structures capable of outwitting dieters' attempts to eliminate them

FAT FREE:
  (e.g. "fat free" cheese) a food-like substance that is rubbery, chewy, and low in taste yet consumed in unnatural amounts by dieters

FOOD COP:
  Person who watches everything eaten and interrogates dieter i.e. "Should you be eating that?" Appropriate response: "Don't you have you own life?"

GUILT:
  Motivating reason to eat to excess *(see also STRESS, ANGER, BOREDOM, HAPPINESS, FRUSTRATION…)*

HUNGER:
  Theoretical physiological state; rarely experienced but more prevalent in presence of

French Fries or fresh, warm, donuts

I'LL JUST HAVE ONE BITE:
Last statement made prior to three weeks of self-induced weight gains

NO THANK YOU, I'M FULL:
No such expression

PETITE:
Size not found in nature *(see also "sizes one through six")*

PORTION:
One unit of food, varies by nutrient - i.e. one portion of vegetables is a tablespoon. One portion of chips is a family size bag.

SCALE:
*^$#*Y#$#@! *(Need I say more?)*

TOMORROW:
Appropriate date to begin dieting *(synonyms: "Next Monday", "January 1st", and "when things settle down")*

WILLPOWER:
Fleeting state of consciousness, usually occurring when clothes are too tight but dissipating quickly in presence of celebrations or chocolate

---

Waiting for Motivation

You stand on the scale, afraid to look. You don't want to know the results because the dreaded "lost your motivation" monster has devoured you. "If I only knew how to get back my motivation, I could get going again."

Many think motivation *leads* behavior and if we lose it, we will never reach our goals. The reality is it does not disappear, we send it away. We can bring it back.

Picture "motivation": empowering, exciting, fearless. It's "lead, follow, or get out of the way." When motivated, nothing prevents us from storming the castle. Yet motivation seems so fickle, disappearing on a moment's notice.

When we start to change a habit, we are not motivated. Instead, usually we are depressed, angry, or forced. Whatever you call it, "motivation" would not be the label. Yet, we give it the old college try "one more time;" anything to get rid of the inner chorus of doubt and self-disgust. We change our behaviors - for whatever reason.

At the end of week one, lo and behold, weight loss! That feels pretty darn good. So, we "give it another week." And again, more weight loss. Energy is rising. Clothes are looser. The sun seems brighter. Things are definitely on the move. Notice the attitude now: motivated!

The point is motivation did NOT lead the behaviors; it *followed* it. When one feels lost, don't look for motivation, start a behavior. Actions lead to motivation.

It's hard to stay vigilant. But it's easier if we don't try and do *everything*, just *one* thing. Choose the first idea that comes into your head and simply do MORE of it, not ALL of it.

Walk five minutes more than you did last week. Stop eating 20 minutes earlier. Make a commitment to do it *right now*. And notice the feeling after you start.

It doesn't take long for motivation to return. It just takes a willingness to do something to invite it back.

Dear Diary

SUNDAY

My backside looks like cottage cheese during an earthquake. Tomorrow, I go on a diet. Here's to success!

MONDAY

I'll start Tuesday. We had treats in the house and had to get rid of them. In retrospect, it might have been smarter to throw them away instead of eat them but what can you do? At least the house is clean of fatty foods, giving me a running start tomorrow. Here's to success!

TUESDAY

So far, so good! No cravings. No slip-ups. We'll see how it goes after I get out of bed. I think I'm going to make it.

WEDNESDAY

My alarm didn't go off so I didn't exercise - but I did try on five pairs of sweat pants to see which looked best. Now, I'm really set for tomorrow. Watch out world!

THURSDAY

The sweats weren't clean; can't exercise in dirty gym clothes so I put that off until tomorrow. In other diet news, I got an order of fries on my way home. At first I felt bad, but then I realized potatoes are vegetables so I got a larger order. This dieting thing isn't so hard.

FRIDAY

Finally got to exercise! I walked to the coffee shop down the block and got a chocolate chip muffin to replace all the calories I burned. Later, the family went to a Mexican restaurant. I realized I might be eating a little much when the waiter brought a fourth basket of chips. So to compensate, I had two light beers instead of regular ones. I don't understand why people complain about diets; this is easy. You just need to think about what you do.

SATURDAY

What a busy day! Between running the kids around, going to the mall, and house cleaning, I'm surprised I had time to breathe. About 4:00, I realized I hadn't eaten so I did three rounds of samples in the grocery store. The amounts they give are so little, there's no way I put on weight. Tomorrow, I get on the scale. I can't wait!

SUNDAY

Dieting doesn't work! I've been perfect all week and - can you believe I gained two pounds?! What's that about?! I'm going to figure out a new plan and start again tomorrow. Right now I have to go; we're late for pizza.

Life in ten-minute segments

I've decided to give you, faithful reader, the "secret solution" to long-term weight loss.

Write this down:

EAT LESS.

Wish there was another way? Yeah, me too.

Anyone who's ever had to lose more than three pounds knows not to eat as much. Despite what screaming tabloids and infomercials promise, calories in versus calories out is the ONLY formula for weight loss (or gain). It is simple math. So why is applying it so far from simple?

Take typical overloaded, stressful, demanding life. Blend in children, husband, bills, shopping, housework, and job. Fold in timetables, schedules, deadlines, and appointments. At day's end, I KNOW I need to eat less; I just don't WANNA (said in my best whiny inner child voice, while stomping my feet). What I WANT is to collapse on the couch with a six-pack and a bag of chips. I'll schedule dieting tomorrow; please make an appointment.

Weight loss (as all things important) requires balance between KNOWING what to do to and WANTING to do it at the same time. Our pesky kicker is that knowledge and desire travel at different velocities. Thoughts plod; urges zoom. Before one can say, "unhand that potato chip," the bag is emptied, the belly is stuffed, guilt struts its victory march. Bringing up the rear, after the damage has been done, we finally stop and think.

Overcoming this inherent psychological unfairness requires leveling the playing field. It's not required to have one's brain engaged full-time. (After all, what fun would there be in reality TV?) What is necessary is slowing the spin during "those" moments. Break the chain; take a short walk. Remember to breathe. The world will continue to revolve without our direction for just a few moments.

At the onset, time crawls. The ugly monster of craving is a fierce competitor, fighting relentlessly for attention. Then dawns the miracle: ah, those wonderful distractions! Urges fade, desires change, ten minutes become an hour, one small notch on my (now smaller) belt of success.

Life – and weight loss – is a parade of ten-minute fragments. Not all go as planned. Yet magic blossoms when we get the current one to go a tiny bit better.

If you think about it – that's all we can do.

Celebrating The Small

Please share with me a moment of silence for my shiny white laptop computer - something about RAM, PMUs, and a logic board. All I know is that it involves major inconvenience, excessive expense, and a whole heap of swearing (um, from me, not the computer). This, as they say, is life.

To alleviate such emotional turmoil, I scout the kitchen in search of rations to a) make me feel better and b) heal my computer. Vegetables accomplish neither. Ice cream scores one; that's better than zero. Decision made, diet jettisoned. (A Nobel Prize is mine I'm sure, if I can figure out the nexus between silicon chips and potato chips.)

We label foods "good" and "bad" as if nutrients had moral degrees, and in swallowing the ingredients, we assume their value. "I am bad for eating the chocolate," screams my inner critical parent. I should know better than that by my age.

I seek to calm the emotional storm by ingesting more, as if the crunching and chewing can drown the thoughts. It is to no avail; the gale rages unappeased, safe harbor is lost. Tonight is lost tonight; I must wait until tomorrow for repairs. Where's that cake?

If guilt and shame were motivational, we'd all be skinny. To the contrary, it is vital that humiliation be banished. We all slide. We fall. The climb to Wisdom is gradual.

To improve I must achieve satisfaction in the knowledge that I now recover faster and harm my efforts less often. When compared to an unrealistic expectation of the perfect dieter, I am doomed to fall short. Without change, I will again eat to medicate that sadness. Overeating leads to guilt that withers into sadness. Such are the fascinating these cycles that drive our lives.

No matter how one spins it, a box of cereal and a pound of Swiss cheese at 10PM is not a healthy way to eat. Yet, reminding myself that what I used to do weekly, I now do monthly, generates a faint beacon of encouragement. A leaky raft still saves more dreams than a rusty weight.

Celebrating miniscule successes can be a slow path to health. But it is assured that beating oneself up doesn't work at all.

Justice Served

"How do you plead?" demands the blaringly bright bold LED screen on the floor scale. The panel flashes "0-0-0" taunting me to stand upon the platform if I dare. Scale knows all; it sees my hidden places. Decision are at hand.

It is my rationale that those who design diets recognize they're working with folks who are fond of eating. (No duh.) Logically then, they must include an unpublished (but common knowledge) "fudge factor" (pun not intended - or maybe it is). It is my assignment to find this limit.

For example, since childhood I was taught to "clean my plate" because "children in Africa were starving." I never understood how my spotless dishes helped others across the globe, but being a youngster, I obeyed. As an adult interested in a healthier global community, I now also clean my son's plate and wife's plate. Oft times, I have toyed with cleaning the plates of diners in the restaurant, but - so far - have resisted.

Since confessions are on the table, I admit that maybe those "couple of tastes" when making cookies would make clear why my recipes yield only 14 cookies - instead of the 24 promised by the cookbook. (I always assumed cookbook editors simply prefer undersized cookies.) Then there's licking the frosting around the perimeter of unused birthday cake. It's unthinkable that would add up, especially when it's well-known that calories migrate to the center.

"Spillage consumption," is another transgression. You know, when emptying cereal (as an example) into a bowl and the "over-pour" spills on to the table. It is unhealthy and bad etiquette to replace it into the carton.

Prospects for bites, licks, and tastes proliferate: the sad, final, pair of broken crackers stranded in the box, a remaining dollop of ice cream in its carton, a quick swallow of soda covering the bottom of the two-liter jug. It drives me off my rocker when others put back an unusable smidgen of a container into the fridge or pantry! In the interest of domestic sanity, I am compelled to nibble.

I reflect on my diet, no longer confident of the verdict. The scales of justice - or more accurately, the justice of the scales - wait to make its pronouncement. I request a recess and leave the room to eat.

Eat Well, Brush Often

Today I share a cautionary tale of danger and woe encountered along the rocky road to healthy eating. Heed my advice, lest ye fall victim to the same trap.

As I lost weight, I expected pitfalls such as slow weight loss or crankiness (due to constricted chocolate consumption). I was caught off-guard by higher dental bills.

Please know me better. As unlikely as the comparison, I'm anal-retentive about oral health. With the money I spent on my last series of dental adventures, I could have single-handedly revived our economy. I have willed my teeth to my wife - as they are the most expensive items I possess. Thusly, to protect these valuable investments, I brush and floss with hyper-regularity.

Still, I find myself visiting the dentist due to an eye-watering stab when I chew on anything with more substance than strained peas. Waiting in the dental chair - noting how much the room looks like an executioner's chamber - I try to will away the toothache with positive thoughts of zero-calorie cheese and peanut butter that flattens abs.

I'm transported out of my fantasy as my dentist enters the room, studying my x-rays. "You obviously have good oral hygiene…" he starts.

I detect a "but" coming. Jeez, I hate "buts."

It hits. "…But you have cavities in your back teeth. Do you eat a lot of sweets?"

"No." I make clear I've lost 70 pounds and eat a balanced diet, high fiber foods and complex carbohydrates.

"Oh," he says. "That explains it. Make sure to brush extra carefully with carbohydrates. They turn to sugar and attack the dentine, causing decay. Eat more protein too."

"But protein is higher in fat. I'll gain weight," I explain as he prepares to excavate.

Ironic, isn't it? I've lost the weight that always plagued me by eating healthier. Yet I'll lose my teeth if I'm not careful. My option is to eat as I did and have healthier teeth - but die early of a cholesterol-induced, weight-related heart attack.

A morbid vision invades my thoughts. Mourners are filing past my casket, commenting between sobs, "It's tragic he died so young - and that he put on all his weight again. But, wow, he sure did have great teeth.

What's Hunger Got to do With it?

As I mindlessly consume my bag of 94% fat-free, 100% taste-free popcorn, my TV-remote surfing pauses at a late-night infomercial touting the latest secret cure in fighting obesity. Were I not so tired, I might question what cruel individual kept it concealed, and why. However, I confess my logic centers were closed for the evening.

I can tell the over-excited announcer is skinny; so much energy at midnight must be a function of high metabolism. He pitches with uncontained enthusiasm: Eat everything you want, no exercise. Change nothing. Swallow this supplement. Lose something like 300 pounds the first fifteen minutes and 25 pounds an hour thereafter!

Yeah, right - and I could flap my arms and fly, if it were not for the buttery salt all over them.

Explaining the apparent contradiction with nutritional science advanced by the pill's miraculous assertions, the voiceover continues, "New LIE-TO-YOUR-FACE FAT-B-GON suppresses your hunger gene so you don't eat. Weight falls off like magic!"

OK, you caught me. I did alter the name of the product for truth-in-advertising purposes. That however misses my point.

Those of us who are overweight consume mass quantities of food even when NOT hungry. I can tell by your now ashen complexion that you are shocked. Alas, 'tis true. When I am unbuttoning my pants at Thanksgiving dinner to thrust another pound of mashed potatoes into my expanding, aching gullet, I left hunger in the rear-view mirror long ago. You would think decent diet researchers might have noticed this.

Hunger is not the issue; my eating is rarely associated with lack of food. So fancy schmancy diet company - suppress my "hunger gene". If I even had such a thing, I think doctors removed it with my tonsils years ago, right before feeding me three day's worth of ice cream.

Should your researchers be truly interested in assisting, I have requests. Suppress my appetite gene; that will help. Or what about my gee-I'm-bored-so-I'll-eat-anything-I-can-stick-a-fork-in gene? Better yet, get rid of that pesky I-had-a-rough-day-so-I-will-consume-a-pound-of-chocolate-and-six pack-of-beer gene.

Come up with one of those puppies and I'll pay $19.95 plus shipping. You won't even have to throw in the Ginsu knives.

The Next Hit TV Show

The siren call of fame and fortune beckon from Southern California. I am convinced that a Hollywood mogul soon will bathe me in riches and adulation to serve as executive producer of my new reality TV series targeted at those of us forever fighting a growing midsection. Love ya baby. Have your people call mine and we'll do lunch. Well, maybe we'll do salad.

The theme? "Outgrow – Outweigh – Outwit."

Here's the treatment. We all know that the more time pants hang in the far reaches of the closet, the increased likelihood they will be too small when we try them on at a later date. Those extra few nibbles from our kid's plate, grocery store samples, and late night snacks, are completely unrelated to our trousers increased tightness. Therefore, it stands to reason that NOT wearing an article of clothing over a long period makes it shrink. Examine the garment label; I'm sure it's in the fine print.

So, work with me here. Based on that concept, I see a human drama occurring each morning while the internal debate of what to wear rages. Instead of eating bugs or jumping from buildings - with heart pounding in our ears - we enter the most fearsome part of the closet; that dark, dank, dusty section where outfits we will "get back into one of these days" hang sadly forgotten. Using jumpy, grainy, hand-held, cinema-verity techniques, our POV is a plentiful plethora of peacoats and paisley pants. Tension escalates and drums pound as the contestant MUST wear the VERY FIRST pair of slacks he touches! Excuses are barred; explanations such as "last night's dinner was a special celebration" carry no water with the waistline referee. One will be voted out of the closet for comments such as, "I'll wait until I lose a few pounds before I try this one" or "that's odd, they fit last week."

With any challenge, there must be rules. Holding in your stomach to tighten the belt: acceptable. Lying on the bed to fasten the zipper: you're fired!

Oh wait, I haven't even told you about the part where they eat the disgusting foods. How about lettuce without salad dressing for a starter?

A Happier Health Plan

I had a "health scare" Friday night. I have decided it's not major – now that I've reclaimed my scattered wits. However, when I change how the Universe works, edict number one proclaims "No health scares prior to long weekends." Mortality is jarring enough without the added anxiety of waiting 72 hours to hear from your doctor. Of course, being a professional-class worrywart, I exacerbate the condition by jumping to the conclusion that I possess a rare tropical ailment. (I am unsure why "tropical" maladies are more horrific than their "temperate" counterparts, yet I remained convinced they are.)

To deal with the anxiety of waiting, I opted for self-treatment as the primary course of action - seeming more appropriate than abject panic. In lieu of a more medically nuanced approach I chose "alternative medicine"; taking the form of several muffins, a lake of ice cream, and a truckload of cookies. (Every treatment has side effects; in this situation, it is a new expanded version of myself.)

Philosophical consideration: why isn't "comfort food" healthier? Imagine the benefits of lowering stress by eating cabbage. Picture a world where one medicates unpleasant feelings with celery or lettuce: a peaceful calmer self –

and a flattering new figure. We can dream, can't we?

Or envision an alternative more fanciful universe. After a doctor's exam for a pesky sore throat, she would pull her Rx pad from her white coat pocket and (with poor penmanship) write upon the paper: "Glacies Cremor Chocolate Yum-Yummis." (For those who skipped Latin, rough translation: "Chocolate Ice Cream.")

"Call this in to the grocery store," she would advise. "Take one gallon three times a day. You get six refills. Take it until you've finished the entire treatment to avoid a relapse. If you miss a dose, take twice as much. And no generics, only the rich, expensive stuff, OK?" Really now, wouldn't that be more healing than some scratchy tasting crimson syrup which evokes a gag reflex?

Marshmallow cookies would heal pulled muscles. French Fries would alleviate heartburn. For serious ailments we would be required to sit in front of the TV and eat an entire family-size jar of peanut butter mixed with chocolate syrup.

Eating My Words

I'd be thinner if I were less popular. I seem incapable of meetings without food; my only venues for talking being "over coffee," "grabbing a bite," or the ever popular "doing lunch." Neither speaker nor writer, instead I have become a professional "luncher;" eating from conference to gathering via restaurant, bar, and restroom.

A finely honed athlete, years of experience have taught me pacing to avoid burn out:

Morning, 8:45: Matt
Discuss marketing. Coffee with half and half. Sugar. Bagel, cream cheese; light.

11:30 AM: Kathy
Negotiations. Coffee. Creamer. Sweetener. Biscotti. (Sample of her croissant; no calories since it's not from my plate.)

Lunch, 12:45: Wife
Emotional connection. Salad. Diet soda (two straws).

2:30 PM: Bob
Vendor. Coffee; decaf! Non-fat milk. Cookie; low fat (tastes like cardboard).

Late afternoon, 4:30: Alan
Advertising. Water. Macaroon. (Leave early to get home in time for dinner.)

I propose a healthier, thinner social climate. Imagine Jeff and I decide to "do talk" at the new Verbalarium in Old Towne; having chose this locale due to its reasonable cost (none of those $5 words). After being seated, an eloquent, thin young employee approaches our table with an order pad in his pocket.

"Gentlemen, what will it be?"

"What's the mot du jour?" I inquire about the special. I've never actually order the special – but I figure someone's doing something exceptional. They need to know people are interested.

"Fresh mixed verbs; transitive and intransitive – our linguist spiced them up with some peppy adverbs."

"Nah, too much action. I'm tired."

"The dictionary special is excellent, fresh from Oxford; nouns, a whole sampler of adjectives, even an exclamation or two. Full variety lets you discuss work, politics, sports - even feelings."

"Feelings? We're male."

"How about an ala Carte platter of partial sentences with a few grunts?"

Fellow seekers of the scale: join with me. In concert we shall revolutionize the social eating norm! Pledge to meet at the mall, connect at the college, or link up at the library. United, our collective (articulate) voices will raise the consciousness and lower the collective waist size of society. The movement is upon us; our first gathering is next week at the local pub.

Putting it in Perspective

Thin people are not "better" people.

Make no mistake; I am burst-my-buttons proud about my extensive weight loss. Yet I am not a superior soul because of it. I have met many who have filled my eyes and heart with beauty and pleasure. Some are slender. Others are not. No correlation is to be found. Restated, the amount of space I occupy on this planet has nothing to do with my worth. Should I be a thoughtless buffoon at 273 pounds, a thoughtless buffoon in a smaller pair of pants is what I shall be when the scales tip at only 138.

Conversely, my ruminations are not a klaxon call for relinquishing self-control; restraint in the pursuit of wellbeing blossoms into pride. As its counterpoint, overindulgence causes our hearts to weep, shunning life, playing less, sulking more in shadows than shining in the sun. Retaining painful behaviors is a squandering of our days. Change can be cleansing.

But reality is that each and every person has embarrassing, annoying, painful - sometimes hurtful habits. We attempt to bury their tracks but they eventually unearth. Being imperfect leaves a lot of loose ends.

So, here's the thing: As one of millions who battles weight, I am neither lazy nor slovenly. My habit is I eat inappropriately. Period. End of story. The only dissimilarity from most others' routines is mine agonizingly broadcasts its result in public. Others' faults can be locked in closets; mine is worn in full view.

If each being were forced to display his or her flaws glaringly on a sign, overweight folks would be overlooked folks. Picture a grandfatherly gentleman with placard above his head emblazoned: "I still sneak cigarettes even though my lungs resemble asphalt." Behind him, a well-heeled woman: "Excuse my mood today. I'm hung-over yet again."

The parade of personal billboards would be endless: "My finances are a mess." "I can't keep a job." "I cheat on my spouse." Without these announcements, each individual knows only his own - yet everyone reads mine: "I eat too much when bored, tired, or depressed."

Perspective is too easily lost: I am not worse - I am merely different. I am empowered. I can change.

In Pursuit of Perfect Foods

In past dieting experiences, I tried removing all temptation - living a Spartan taste-free subsistence comprised of foodstuffs with a flavor and texture akin to cardboard. While gnawing and slashing my way through tough, rubbery, bland, fibrous food, the thought dawned on me, "If this is what I have to eat to live to be 100, why bother?" As there was no compelling answer, I opt now for more innovative methods to control my weight.

Example: I like pizza. OK, "like" is an extremely meek word for my attraction to this disk-shaped, flat hubcap of gastronomic bliss. To put things in perspective, as much as I adore my spouse - given the choice between a four-cheese, stuffed-crust, sausage-laden, deep-dish, garlic-pepperoni pizza pie and my wife - I would still opt for my wife. But, I gotta tell you, the judging could be close. (Oh dear, I am going to be in so much trouble when I get home tonight…)

I do have limits, only one piece of pizza per sitting - albeit it is a round 16" piece which the restaurant graciously cuts into eight sub-pieces. Usually, the pizza's will dominates my mere mortal sensibilities, forcing me to follow my meal with buffalo wings, cheesy breadsticks dipped in garlic butter, and white chocolate strawberry cheesecake. This ingestion frenzy fogs my senses sending me scouring my environs in search of anything sluggish enough to pierce with a fork. Even my cat becomes rightfully cautious when I'm eyeing her while in one of these moods.

To try and counter these cravings, I founded EATS: Experimental Alternative Tasty Solutions. The ultimate quest is a non-fat, zero-calorie, no net carb, sugarless, no preservative added, guilt-free – yet flavorful - snack. Results have been mixed with some formulas achieving moderate success. Others, such as lettuce dipped in fat-free chocolate syrup, faring less well.

My current project involves a guiltless pizza: One high fiber wheat tortilla, soaked in salsa, sprinkled with fat-free Parmesan cheese, low fat cottage cheese, and garlic. Granted, there are doubters, but I am expecting to have it in several restaurants immediately after I market my dieter's substitute for spaghetti: boiled bean sprouts covered with ketchup.

In the Interest of Airport Security

With customer service for airlines a forgotten art, referring to travelers as "passengers" is akin to referring to cattle herded in the fields as "pedestrians." As I trudge shoeless and belt-less hither and yon through airport security, I restrain the urge to let loose with a sarcastic "MOOOO." Most likely, there is a regulation about exhibiting bovine behaviors while going through security.

I will concede some improvements. Our local airport used to inquire how much we weighed during check-in. My presumption is this practice ceased due to loss of customers; some of us will walk to New York rather than fly if it involves announcing our weight in front of strangers. Religion. Politics. Body mass index: topics not to be discussed with uniformed personnel recording information in computers.

Besides, what purpose did it serve? Did the skinniest folks get the package of 13 stale pretzels and 23 peanuts in the event of a severe onboard snack shortage?

Yet, I remember the quandary of deciding what weight to state. Untruths about weight on a driver's license are different; who resembles their license photo? Airplanes are different. If it wasn't vital for the pilot to have accuracy, they would just add up the weight listed on everyone's licenses. Since it's common knowledge that's not even within flying distance of accurate, it is safe to assume my mass is related to airline safety. Should my fib be too extensive, the humiliating headline in tomorrow's paper would shout: JET FALLS FROM SKY BECAUSE SCOTT LIES ABOUT HIS WEIGHT.

So, I ponder "massaging" the number; a few ounces won't hurt. After all, my jeans weigh more than if I wore shorts. Simply because I live in a colder climate, I should not be penalized. Paranoia takes hold: What happens if everyone thought this way? Underpowered, the plane would be unable to achieve lift off, therefore rolling down the freeway all the way to its destination.

I imagine a conversation in an auto on highway 101 as it passes the Boeing 707 in the right lane:

"Honey, there's a plane driving next to us."

"Don't worry; just a bunch of passengers who lied about their weight."

"Oh. That would explain why they're all eating diet snacks."

Burning it Off

If I exercised more, I'd weigh twice what I do now. Let me explain.

Working alone in an office frequently leads to feelings of loneliness and boredom. Feelings of loneliness and boredom habitually lead to eating. Alas, if those were the only feelings that led to eating, this saga would have a happy ending. Regrettably for me, eating is also triggered by stress, happiness, sadness, excitement, confusion, fear, anxiety… well, you get the point.

To handle this stew of emotions, I periodically remove myself from the choir of internal voices taunting, "A snack will help you focus." Should that be truthful - and if I heeded their advice as often as suggested - I would be extremely focused, but would no longer fit in my chair. For that reason I opt to engage in a bike ride to accomplish a few errands; the effect being I can replace feeling plump with feeling proud.

As they say, it seems like a good idea at the time.

Stop one: warehouse outlet. After my transaction, I reward myself with a frozen yogurt before continuing to the video store. My DVD securely deposited in the slot, I withdraw a quarter from my pocket and insert it in the candy machine, turning slowly to make sure I get the full bounty of colorful candies that will not melt in my hand but definitely dissolve in my mouth, fortifying me for my two-block walk to the supermarket. After purchasing a few groceries, my first order of business is to rummage through the white plastic bag and remove candied, dried, fruit – a treat for my return stroll. Strapping the provisions atop my bike rack; I stop to fill my tires with air – and my belly with cinnamon jelly candies, finalizing this rolling feast with an energy bar from the mini-mart, assuring I shan't collapse from exhaustion on the final leg of my journey.

Four stops and five desserts later, I excuse myself with the mantra, "I burned it all off." The reality is to burn off all I consumed, I'd have to outperform Lance Armstrong in the tour de France. Undeterred and proud of my exercise, I return to my office - wondering why I didn't lose weight this week.

Unexpected & Unpleasant Realities

Nancy was younger than I am. Although we had no recent contact, I grieve. You will be missed. Rest well.

Mortality is a pair of tight shoes, poorly fit, pinching, wearable; less comfortable over years. I find methods to protect myself from unpleasant realities; some feelings and sentiments can be too messy.

Shield of choice? Yeah, you guessed it - food. I react to this sad information by trying to strip away my unpleasant feelings by the light of a 15-watt refrigerator bulb. If I inspect these chilly confines long enough, the perfect comfort food might miraculously appear. Devoid of calories and their pesky side effects, it will purify me of sorrow. Hunger is not what is driving me on my search; calmness through this emotional maelstrom is my mission. Who's to say it isn't stored in the cold crisper section?

As a grown-up, I "know" this quest is futile. Cartons of ice cream, or cold six-packs are no cure for what frightens me. As I said, as a grown-up, I know.

However, I think I missed the turn-off to adulthood.

Although periodically enlightened with the insights of years, mostly the world seems as it did when I put playing cards in bicycle spokes and battled invisible invaders in my back yard. I still feel so new. With the exception of some grey hairs and a few lines, maybe aging will pass me by.

Reality barges in, unannounced, uninvited, at the most inopportune moments. I have too much to do right now; could we schedule this breakdown for later? So, being a child, I attempt to avoid this icky-ness. "Make it go away," is my oft-repeated mantra and I do so by eating, a cookie (or more) to heal my boo-boo.

The irony is although so comforting in the immediate; over-indulgence propels me deeper into a vortex of despair. By running from, I run toward.

Refrigerator still open, feelings stop cascading long enough for a breath. Worry is interest on a debt not yet owed; stay in the present. A Herculean effort, I force shut the refrigerator. The pressure of sadness is not gone but cleaner. This moment, I force myself to focus on Life. I will remember her better - and be healthier - when I take a moment to smile.

Negotiations with the Scale

I am unusually gifted. I can convert my thoughts to rationalize eating just about anything, while convincing myself it will help me lose weight.

Reading the diet program booklet, I find: "One cup strawberries, large."

Analyzing the situation, I look for the letter of the law, not deterred by its spirit. "It doesn't say what size is a 'cup'." I ponder the philosophical possibilities. "Isn't a bucket really just a *very large cup*?" Nodding to no one in particular, I am pleased with this obviously overlooked understanding of the program's intent.

But why stop there? Strawberries leave spaces between them. Surely, my diet doesn't expect me to count the air between! After all, no weight loss program worth its salt wouldn't want me to sacrifice the valuable nutrients found in fruit by including the spaces.

A light flashes in my food-deprived brain. "Jam! If I fill the cup (or bucket as the case might be) with strawberry jam, there is no 'inter-berry, nutritionally-voided' space! Wow, am I brilliant! Dieting is easy. This is great!"

Exaggerated example? Sure. Yet it begs the larger question. "If the program leads me to health, happiness, and admiration from others, why do I so readily 'negotiate terms' and look for 'loopholes' that will only lead me away from my goals?

The scale is an unforgiving master, caring not for measurements and rationales. All is knows is what I weigh, a reflection of my actions – a real-world representation of feelings and thoughts.

When faced with internal negotiation of the terms of my diet, I need to compare both sides. One choice gives me an opportunity to feel better and healthier for a long time. The other gives me immediate satisfaction - followed by a hard-crashing plate of guilt and disappointment.

I have a long-term goal to improve my life. I can delay my arrival in this Promised Land - or I can speed it up. That choice presents itself often and regularly. Keeping positive feelings in the forefront of my mind's eye helps me choose success more times than not.

I can always turn around later.

Disarming the Food Bomb

A diet is walking a minefield. At times, the path seems clearly marked and I skirt each temptation. Yet, there are THOSE days. KERBLAM! All is lost.

Recently, I had one of "those days." The universe was in perfect order until - out of the blue - I resemble an ad for cold remedies. Sneezing. Coughing. Teary eyes.

I am not a good patient; I go from pleasant to cranky in nothing flat. To soothe myself, I eat. No minor league consumption for me. I'm a professional. (Don't try this at home.) I inhale a box of sugary cereal, granola bars, a few little tiny frozen quiches, popcorn, and ice cream. I was medicating my soul not my body.

Logically, that makes no sense. Yet if you're reading this column, you probably have more than a passing interest in weight loss. I'm sure you've been in the same place.

In my "old days," that event could have set me back months. Though black and white lens, I would have seen this "food explosion" as further proof that I was *completely* incapable of losing weight. Internal Nag would have cackled, "You blew it *again*! No willpower. Give up already." Indeed I heeded that advice countless times, delaying my weight loss for years.

Reality is I cannot avoid "food bombs" completely. Food happens. The definition of "Success" is to have these "explosions" less often - with less damage - and recover faster from the effects. If I get back on track in a day – instead of a month – that's amazing progress! If my binges consist of cereal instead of muffins, more progress. Once a month instead of once a week is a 400% improvement.

I still strive to improve but progress is not linear. It has forward – and backward – movement. Expecting perfection only sets myself up for failure by establishing unrealistic expectations. The irony being that when I inevitably do "fail," I eat to soothe myself.

Focus on how much you've improved, not what is yet to be learned. That instills a sense pride, which does far more to accomplish goals than will shame and guilt.

Thanksgiving Diets

"Please pass another heaping pound of mashed potatoes soaking in gravy and butter."

It sure seems that the next five weeks are a license for gluttony. Ads tout indigestion medicines by the bucketful. People *boast* about how sick they got from eating too much. Some even don "ceremonial garb" for the turkey meal: loose clothes, no belt, and elastic waistlines.

How does one make it through Thanksgiving without falling "off the wagon" while still enjoying the celebration?

The key is NOT to give up all one's favorite foods. Indeed that triggers feelings of deprivation, abandonment, anger, and loneliness; all of which generate the urge to eat even more.

Instead, success means learning how to control the causes of overeating. Some simple, quick, (relatively) painless suggestions include:

Use a smaller plate. Visual cues are a major trigger of overeating. In other words, if there's room on the plate, we'll fill it with food. Smaller plates fill us up mentally.

Before putting anything else on your plate, fill half of it with vegetables. Use the remainder for the "other stuff."

Wait at least ten minutes from the time the thought crosses your mind until you reach for seconds (or thirds). Don't worry; there will be more. After all, have you ever been to a Thanksgiving meal where there wasn't *enough* food?

Drink lots of water before each meal. And then drink more. If you don't feel like a walking lake, you need more water.

Don't expect to be as regimented this time of year as you would be the remainder of the year. Be kind to yourself when you slip but don't "wait until January" before getting back on track. A few days of carelessness generates only a few pounds. A month will generate far more, making your return that much more difficult.

Realize the reason for the holiday. Be thankful for blessings given, not food consumed. It is one of the greatest blessings to be in control of one's health. Take a moment to remember that.

Following a diet during the "eating season" does not have to demote one to meals of carrot sticks and water. It can be a joyful time of year no matter how much one eats.

Dieting, Salads, and the Hotel Bathroom

After speaking in Chicago last weekend, I went in search of a healthy meal to bring to my hotel room. From the local convenience store, I bought what was advertised as a "Delicious Garden Fresh Deluxe Vegetable Salad" (in its own plastic finery).

Wanting to avoid spilling the small plastic package of fat free dressing, I utilized the only sink I could find: in my bathroom. "After all," I mused, "aren't all the finest meals prepared over a bathroom sink?"

The hospitality industry has not come to grips with an overweight country. (To be fair, we aren't pushing very hard either.) I can buy bottled water in my room; but if gasoline were the same price per ounce as that water, I'd be paying $24 a gallon for fuel! Fruit? How about plunking out $2 for a mealy, squishy, tasteless red apple or bruised banana. Aside from these "healthy" choices, a traveler can choose muffins, scones, fried animal parts (not known in nature), soda – or the aforementioned, very expensive – unceremoniously prepared – "deluxe" salad.

Being as concerned about my wallet as I am about waistline, my tendency was to order the greasy, crunchy, gooey, fried things – and start my diet again when I got home. For years, I did that. During that same period, I put on weight. Coincidence? I think not.

Now, I try to remind myself I'm worth the cost. If it were anyone else in my family needing a few extra bucks for their health, I'd have it in an instant. I use the money as an excuse to keep my old habits. Truth be told, if eating well staves off even one weight-related medical procedure, I will have saved thousands. (And how does one count the value of a positive attitude that comes from taking care of oneself?)

I'm not perfect on the road but I am more conscious. I shop at local grocery stores for more healthful choices. I bring my own snacks. I don't "supersize." I won't bring extra food into my room. (I do draw the line at eating those lousy apples.)

Is my way successful? I'll find out when I weigh in this week. But of one thing I can be sure, the old way of traveling sure wasn't.

Waiting for Motivation

You stand on the scale, afraid to look. You don't want to know the results because the dreaded "lost your motivation" monster has devoured you. "If I only knew how to get back my motivation, I could get going again."

Many think motivation *leads* behavior and if we lose it, we will never reach our goals. The reality is it does not disappear, we send it away. We can bring it back.

Picture "motivation": empowering, exciting, fearless. It's "lead, follow, or get out of the way." When motivated, nothing prevents us from storming the castle. Yet motivation seems so fickle, disappearing on a moment's notice.

When we start to change a habit, we are not motivated. Instead, usually we are depressed, angry, or forced. Whatever you call it, "motivation" would not be the label. Yet, we give it the old college try "one more time;" anything to get rid of the inner chorus of doubt and self-disgust. We change our behaviors - for whatever reason.

At the end of week one, lo and behold, weight loss! *That* feels pretty darn good. So, we "give it another week." And again, more weight loss. Energy is rising. Clothes are looser. The sun seems brighter. Things are definitely on the move. Notice the attitude now: motivated!

The point is motivation did NOT lead the behaviors; it *followed* it. When one feels lost, don't look for motivation, start a behavior. Actions lead to motivation.

It's hard to stay vigilant. But it's easier if we don't try and do *everything*, just *one* thing. Choose the first idea that comes into your head and simply do MORE of it, not ALL of it.

Walk five minutes more than you did last week. Stop eating 20 minutes earlier. Make a commitment to do it *right now*. And notice the feeling after you start.

It doesn't take long for motivation to return. It just takes a willingness to do something to invite it back.

Does This Make Me Look Fat?

After decades of portliness, it is sometimes difficult to believe I am no longer so. Even with a waistline of 33, I approach grocery store turnstiles sideways, lifting my belly to pass over what appears too-narrow access. I instinctively gravitate to "large men's" clothing. "Does this make me look fat?" leaves my lips with such regularity; I should tattoo it on my forehead.

In pursuit of an accurate self-image, I contrast how clothes fit me with other men I observe. Nothing is wrong with women's fashions; it is merely that such apparel would fit poorly on a person of my proportions and I might look heftier. However, if lacy, frilly, and pink, should look slimming, I wouldn't necessarily rule it out.

The cultural norms of the American male however, require discretion. My gender rarely approaches one another with observations such as, "Those pants look quite flattering on you. Can I feel the fabric?" Fabric fondling is a major masculine faux pas.

Adjacent to me in line at the coffee house is a well-appointed gentleman of similar stature and age. Noticing his reflection in the window, I wonder, "Do I look that thin?" To unravel such a mystery, I make use of all the poise, grace, and discretion of a clumsy, middle-age guy with a befuddled body image, and attempt to discreetly put side by side our reflections. Unaware he is observing me, I compare waist sizes, posture, and accessories (such as men have).

Now is where it gets strange.

Because my arms are crossed over my chest, I notice I can feel my ribs. To heavy people, bones are theoretical. Actually proof of existence is an infrequent indulgence worth savoring, so forgetting where I am, my fingers begin caressing my side, counting bones - an explorer in a new land.

The man's eyes and mine meet for a moment - one extremely long, awkward, laboriously painful embarrassing moment; I am slammed back into reality. Attempting to force a nonchalant smile, my expression instead resembles one of a cat releasing a hairball.

Disappearing through the hardwood floor flashes across my consciousness. Finding that impossible, I quickly opt to leave via the front door, deciding, "who needs coffee anyway?" Yet, as I exit, I can't help but wonder if he's thinking I look thin from behind.

Detours, Diets, Determination

Following a diet can be akin to walking too close to the ragged edge of an unstable cliff.

What starts out as healthy respect for the danger of testing the terrain inevitably devolves to a game of chicken; pushing limits to see much we can challenge before the scale tattles on our sloppiness. Soon, we "help" our children clean their plate by taking "just a small bite" of leftovers. The rationale, "if I eat it over the sink, I burn off the calories" becomes a truism. At dinner, the phrase "please give me the big one" unthinkingly pops out of our mouth. Before one can say "extra large with fries," we tumble into the abyss of abandoned goals and expanding waistlines - yet again.

Reality check: each person who has successfully lost weight has "slipped" repeatedly. The difference lies in the view: they view slippage NOT as "falling off a cliff", but "stumbling along a path."

In any new endeavor, we will - like children acquiring new skills - trip up. We remind our children to get "back on the horse". Yet, for ourselves, we stay firmly planted in the mud, chanting the mantra: "I blew it… (pause to finish mouthful of chips)… As long as I blew it… I might as well really blow it." Then, what would have been just a bag of chips includes a box of cookies, a quart of ice cream, and a jar of peanut butter (followed by diet soda to avoid any damage…).

If the stumble would have terminated at the bag of chips, I might have gained a pound (maybe two). Yet if I look at myself as "over the edge" (instead of "finding my way,") there is no incentive to minimize the damage. Whether I careen down the hill at full or half speed makes no difference, the unpleasant result of hitting bottom is exactly the same. Therefore, I might as well enjoy the fall. I'll start again next week. (Please pass the chocolate…)

Detours happen and, yes, they will indeed delay arrival at the Promised Land. But "delayed" is faster than "never. Dust yourself off and get back on track immediately. You're still on the path.

Bicycles, Missed Appointments, and Habits

I drove my car to an appointment today.

That might not seem noteworthy as I am a member of a way of life that has been known to drive from the bedroom to kitchen. An explanation is therefore in order.

Five years ago, I determined a bicycle would help in my unrelenting quest to lose "those last 10 pounds." I purchased a bright green, shiny, "commuter bike:" just the ticket for errands, short trips — and looking way-righteously cool. With inner child at full throttle, I straddled my 24-speed cycle with headlight, rear LED, bike rack, and "computer" — which, in reality, is a "speedometer on steroids" that cycling folks refer to as a "computer." (Who am I to argue?) Strapping on matching green helmet and bike gloves, I tightened my backpack, adjusted my side mirror, and pedaled away — simply to collapse, exhausted, a mile from home. Remind me again whose bright idea this was.

Each subsequent pedaling opportunity was overruled by geographic or meteorological concerns. In Humboldt County, if one excludes riding in hills, wind, or rain, let's face it; you stay home.

So, after much soul searching (and two more pounds), I ventured into the asphalt wilds for one brief ride. A few blocks one day, more on another, soon I'm across town. Wind? Gear down. Hills? Stand up. For rainy days, I bought yellow raingear (added bonus: look like a banana slug on wheels). Before one could utter, "derailleur," most short outings were via bicycle; soon becoming second nature. Lance Armstrong's record is safe — but big-wheeled, plastic trikes quite often eat my dust.

Back to today: When my faithful two-wheel steed broke, I was disoriented. I had an appointment and no way to get there — until I remembered I still possess a car. From inventing excuses to drive, to forgetting I even owned an auto — there's your lightning bolt moment.

Isn't that the way it is with habits? They begin so small, initially difficult, then awkward, then you. Actions requiring so much energy at their onset evolve into activities unnoticed, as invisible as the thoughts that guide them. One moment. One month. One lifetime, it all blends. Go slowly; just keep moving. You'll get there.

Oh yeah, I fixed my bike. I ride again tomorrow, feels awkward when I don't.

Long Term Relationships

I am blessed. I have a happy marriage with a delightful woman (who accepts my quirks).

It does not come without some effort. Each day is NOT better than the previous day. There are "*those*" days (they seem like weeks) where nothing works between us. In those dark mornings, honesty compels me to admit I have indeed questioned the value of long-term relationships.

There are times that, no matter how much I plead (even beg) for her to see the "wisdom" of my ways - alas, she does not. When I find myself plunged into that sea of emotional muck, I pause, take a deep breath, (feel frustrated, angry, sad) - and then figure out what *I* must do to fix it. It is now up to *me* to change. For me to be happy and achieve my goals, I learn to accept reality while keeping focused on the positives of what I get from my efforts. My wife will do what my wife will do. I will learn how to deal with it. Truth is, I will love her either way for most of what I get, I enjoy.

Our partnership is not unlike most happy "LTRs". A lot of ups. Some dark, painful, downs. Mostly "in-betweens" trending positive. Quite frankly, some days are just downright fantastic.

Weight loss is a long-term relationship. Each day (maybe even each hour) requires renewed commitment - or eventual divorce. I will make mistakes (sigh...). Conversely, the process will not always behave as I wish it would. The question to ask at crossroads: "is this worth ending the relationship?" During those questioning periods, I look long-term, counting seconds until I'm through being "here" - yet realizing "here" happens – and will again.

I must do what *I* can do (resentfully at times), let go of guilt and blame, and realize that any "good" relationship is not always "good," it is "good" *more times than not.*

Losing weight – and sustaining a happy marriage – are not done perfectly. (Just ask my wife!) However, they are worth the work if we're willing to be patient, understanding, and have realistic expectations.

Are We There Yet?

"Can we stop now?"

"No," I sigh. I seem to sigh a great deal these days. "We must keep going."

Comes the reply – always – "Why?"

This does not have an easy answer. What logic exists in following a path with no conclusion? Sometimes, I am unsure why I trudge forever forward toward that golden, sunny, meadow atop the distant mountain. Having labored long and hard, I am fatigued. At these times, I can easily persuade myself to stop my quest. "Just for a short time," I think. I deserve time off.

I announce that I shall "take a short break." My family and friends have been to this site with me repeatedly; loving concern is in their eyes. I assure them (and me), "Don't worry. I'm not giving up; I just need to relax. I'll get back on program in a little while."

In my honest places, I know I will not remain here if I stop; I will regress. "A little while" will become "someday;" "relax" will be "give up." I will tumble again to my beginning, pained, and further from my goal.

This road extends forever; no finish line with cheering crowds awaits. Never will I burst through the tape, my hands raised high above my head. To focus on an end point when none exists invites frustration. No thank you, I already have a surplus.

If I could change my yesterdays, I would do in a flash. Alas, that option is no longer available. I find myself here, nowhere else.

It makes the journey easier to appreciate what I have accomplished, rather than obstacles I will face. The terrain has been rugged; yet the distance I have traveled is still great. Peaceful moments, insightful lessons, and inner satisfaction have blossomed along the way. And when I accept - that despite the work - I am better now than at my start, calmness sweetens the moment.

The hallowed land is not across a future bridge, nor over distant borders. It is within, in the soft, quiet, satisfaction of a small step. With a deep breath (or is it another sigh?) I adjust my focus to the Now and persevere, breathing easier for my lightened load.

Halloween Tricks

Shortly after trick-or-treating, I'd take the stuffed sack of sweetened snacks and methodically commence the annual sorting ritual. First: remove the boring, plain, unimaginative lollipops on white paper sticks. If someone with my heft found them unflavorful, I didn't see how confectionery companies even stayed in business producing them. Vineyards have wine tasting. Don't makers of munchies invest in something similar?

Chocolate bars were meticulously analyzed, classified, and culled from their chewy caramel brethren. Mini bags of jellybeans and foil-wrapped drops were each placed in distinct heaps. When all was it should be, 'twas time to sit back and savor the fruits of my efforts until my teeth ached from sugar, and my belly from bulk.

Oh yes, one other detail: honesty compels me to report that this recollection was not of my own tender years. Rather, as father, when my children would drift off to sleep on Halloween night, I would stealthily claim their plunder, rationalizing they need not suffer cavities nor bellyaches. Denial, combined with the prospect of 17 marshmallow fudge bars, can push one's integrity to the breaking point.

Children scrutinize their candy count in the same manner bankers track investments; so come morning, the inquest begins, "Dad, where's the rest of my candy?"

Having foreseen this, I had deftly spread the cellophane-wrapped bounty across the table, assuming it would appear more sizeable than it really was. "Oh my!" I exclaim, trying to generate contagious enthusiasm. "You've got loads of candy. Look." Alas, this misrepresentation was caused by being under the influence of toffee peanuts; please forgive.

His young piercing blue eyes drilled a hole, making it difficult — but not impossible — to tell untruths. "Um, maybe you spilled some. There could be a hole in the bag." Glancing around agitatedly, I hoped to find the sack and surreptitiously tear loose a small slit as evidence.

"It's a plastic pumpkin container. It can't rip." Undeterred, his cross-examination persisted, "Where is my candy?"

I wanted to come clean, be the good dad. The sugar buzz banging around in my brain made it too difficult. Wiping telltale sugar from my moustache, I opted for one final diversionary tactic. "Actually son, I saved the extra special ones for you. Wouldn't you prefer this great big pile of lollipops?"

Food Police and Other "Diet Assistants"

"Is *that* on your diet?"

There stands the most annoying question I get while losing weight. No matter how carefully worded and lovingly delivered, it always comes across to me as (delivered in the tone of a schoolyard taunt), "Neener-neener-neener! I caught you cheating!"

I admit I have been known to sneak food, not wanting others to know I eat too much. (Of course, with a 44-inch waistline, they probably figured it out for themselves.) Despite my ten-year success at maintaining a 70-pound weight loss, to this day - others commenting on what I eat still triggers strong feelings. (Dare say, enough to make me want to eat!).

When confronted with these benevolent "Food Police," my initial reaction is to share what I'm eating rather forcefully by guiding it to her face. Sad truth dawning, that will not help me accomplish my goal. Moreover, my next meal might be served through bars.

In reality, my questioner ("inquisitor" might be more accurate) is not trying to throw me from my quest, but is (arguably) trying to help me stay focused. She knows I've been down this well-worn path often and feels – with her guidance – she can guide me around the potholes. She desires for me happiness, and therefore intends to "help" me achieve it.

Keeping *that* interpretation in the forefront (difficult as it might be), I not only prevent the urge to hide, but can convert that intention to support. The trick is how I react to the folks who inhabit my eating environs.

Instead of answering the question directly, I RECOGNIZE the *intention*. Putting down the food (removing the white sugary coating from my face), I take a deep breath, calm myself, and reply, "Thank you for helping me stay focused. I appreciate it." I have now avoided time in the correctional facility. Continuing, I REFLECT and REDIRECT. In effect, I tell her how I feel, and give provide a more productive road to assistance: "…However, when you watch what I eat, I feel self-conscious. If you'd like to help, what I could really use is…" (And I give her an idea.)

Food is a social component; we cannot spend all our time alone. Gently guiding the inquisitive, helpful, (albeit nosy) folks who surround us will build better relationships and heightened success.

Hurricane Katrina

This column was not supposed to happen; instead, I was scheduled to be a keynote speaker at a conference in Louisiana this day. Mother Nature had other ideas delivered as hurricane Katrina.

With indescribable sorrow and mouth agape at the sight of such awfulness, I cannot pull myself away from the plight of the Gulf Coast. Robotically, I shake my head and repeat numbly, "There but for the grace of God, go I." It could just as easily have been an earthquake or Tsunami bringing national cameras to scrutinize my family in our most intimate, broken moments struggling to hold together, adrift, frightened, and cold in the worst of all worlds.

Due to the unsympathetic force of nature and the rearrangements being made, I have lost income. Yet compared to my friend and associate, Myra, my costs pale. Where she lived has no roof and is full of water. In spite of that, she describes herself as "fortunate." She spent today helping families with less. I am privileged to know her.

So very fortunate am I that I take blessings as common-day events. When involved in the confines of day-to-day existence, I have been known to whine bitterly about sluggish traffic, jammed faxes, or misplaced keys. Broken shoelaces, missing shirt buttons, or ants on my sink irk me endlessly.

I presume my daily misadventures can indeed be labeled "problems," and yes, they are frustrating. At the same time, reality is they are so insignificant. Too often, I become too self-centered to remember that. The dropped cellular call or the unexpected invoice becomes the world's prime catastrophe. I puff up and spout off, grumbling to my friends, who nod in agreement. We are bonded by our miseries. When we rule the world, things will change.

In a world that can shatter instantly, where unfathomable countless thousands lack shelter, shed tears for loved ones, or cannot find food, I bemoan that I have to count fat grams or cut back on dessert. Can I even know how many pray to be in my shoes?

Peace of mind requires that I remind myself that my tribulations and troubles are usually min-iscule. Put it in perspective. Life is rich. Keep it that way; shut the refrigerator door.

Saying "I Do"

I knew I needed to lose weight a long time before I actually did it. It's not like my expansive waistline was the result of some unthinking, collegiate one-night drinking binge. The morning after, in a head-pounding stupor, I stagger awake exhausted from the previous night's goings on, gawk at the 70 new pounds around my middle and exclaim in shock, "What the heck did I do to myself last night?"

Weight gain is insidiously seductive. A full-frontal attack is not its manner. Rather it catches us in our unawares, sliding on unhurriedly, clinging, hugging, enveloping.

Red flags rise quickly; but just as when that glow fades from a new relationship, I want to overlook the warnings. An added belt notch, a stabbing unfamiliar backache, discomfort wearing my favorite clothes; oh sure, I'm aware of these modifications - too aware - I merely turn away. Change is difficult, unplanned, and just plain unpleasant; deal with it later.

"Tomorrow," becomes my mantra. "Tomorrow, I'll be careful. Tomorrow, I'll be better. Tomorrow…" Promises delayed evolve into promises un-kept. As my grandmother Zlate repeatedly cautioned, "Tomorrow never comes."

Weight gain is a progressive disease; benign neglect begets escalation. What was five pounds is now 25. In order to avoid now-constant back pains, gardening and bending are curtailed. Walking to the corner store is enough to make breathing difficult. Devising reasons to avoid visiting the doctor becomes a full-time occupation. The pleasures of life slip ever further from my grasp.

Dieting - if done well - is in actuality, "improving the connection to one's body," as my body and I share the ultimate long-term relationship. Richer or poorer, for better or worse, in sickness and health, till death do me part.

Even the greatest relationships cause some pain. My marriage counselor reminds me that improvements are not immediate, yielded instead over time. Thoughtful progressions - one foot in front of the other, adjust, back, forward, slide, slip, feel like quitting; all important lessons in the dance.

Perfect dieting is like a perfect marriage: a glorious, intoxicating dream. It is, alas, also unattainable. Nonetheless, setting my sights and moving slowly in that direction is still healthier than standing still and waiting for it to arrive.

Fifty Two

Gratefulness is the kernel from which prosperity grows. For reasons somewhat unclear to me, giving thanks liberates the soul, lifts the spirit, and propels one to elevated levels. It is an enlightening, invigorating — and unfortunately, under-experienced occurrence.

Today's commentary marks our 52nd get-together — one year. That's 19,273 words, 16,083,432 re-writes, and a heck of a lot of newsprint. Anniversaries are an appropriate time to give thanks, so I beg your indulgence.

Despite 16 million articles belaboring carbs, calories, and calisthenics, the great American midsection continues its relentless expansion. We have been lectured to "eat less and exercise more" ad nausea. We KNOW what to do; we're just ignoring it. Being overweight, not stupid, we understand that when loosening our pants to squeeze in a few more scoops of cheesy pasta, it doesn't help the diet. What would lend a hand is how beliefs and feelings are the genesis of said over-indulgence. My notion about a year ago was, "Why doesn't someone write about that?"

As fate would have it, my local newspaper started a weekly health section. I proposed as a column, "a cross between Nutrition 101, therapy, and a southern revival." Upon the editor's gracious (and surprising) acceptance, I became "Someone."

Every Wednesday, I plop down in front of my Macintosh computer, coffee (without sugar) at my side, and compose these missives. I address this experience from only my perspective, as that is all I have. Anything else would be disingenuous. From my place in the front lines of the diet wars, I strive for honesty, transparency, motivation — and hopefully, a seasoning of humor.

I am honored, flattered, and touched by the reaction. I have received emails, letters, postcards, mid-street conversations, articles, books, phone calls, speaking invitations, and attendance in my seminars. You have reinforced that we are all cut of the same cloth: neither broken, damaged, nor inadequate, merely doing what we do as well as we can — just like everyone else. It's refreshing to know.

The power of the printed word is a force of nature and I am so grateful for the access, and even more appreciative that you read this. Thank you for the inspiration and a wonderful premier year; I am in your debt.

Catch you next week with #53.

Need Additional Weight Loss Support?

Scott's website, **www.THINspiration.com**, has loads of FREE information and support. Click on the "weight loss support" link in the upper left corner and find a great deal of support at no charge.

You can also sign up for Scott's FREE motivational e-zine when you're there.

If you'd like a motivational CD or mp3 download about weight loss delivered to a live audience entitled, *"What's Eating You and Why Are you Eating it Back?"* go to the site below.

Anything you order from Scott comes with a 100% money back guarantee. If you don't like it, he'll buy it back.

To order, call toll free 866.762.7287 or visit www.TheEatingCycle.com

CD $15 + $4.50 shipping
MP3 $4.95 + no shipping

Order the CD and get the
174 ideas to Lose Weight
e-Book & the mp3 downloads FREE!

About Scott

Scott "Q" Marcus lost 70 pounds while going through one of the most tumultuous years of his life.

How? He learned the habits he was trying to change were not the "problem"; they were a symptom of a "need-to-be-perfect" belief that holds so many of us back from our true potential. The reality is that small changes made more times than not generate more results than big changes rarely completed. In effect, the pursuit of perfection gets in the way of getting better. Hence: "Strive for Imperfection."

Hundreds come to see him time and time again to share in his THINspirational, playful, energetic delivery polished through an award-winning extensive career of public speaking, performance, radio, television and writing.

His topics, as these columns, are NOT about "carbs and calories;" instead they cover a wide range from conflict management to attitude change to goal setting. Yet, all share an empowering belief in the spirit within.

Scott is a sought-after speaker for health groups, sales organizations, non-profits, and any organization looking for a dynamic speaker with a message delivered in a lively, playful, insightful, fashion.

In addition to being a syndicated columnist, trainer, keynote speaker, and consultant for several organizations, Scott is a professional member of the National Speakers Association and executive producer of "CruiseTheBetterLife.com," a motivational cruise company that produces customized cruises to be used as fundraisers and morale boosters.

Although his topics are NOT necessarily about eating and diet - he does welcome contributions of French Fries or peanut butter.

Scott can be reached for speeches, workshops, of cruise planning at 707.442.6243 or 866.SMARCUS (866.762.7287) or via email at scottq@scottqmarcus.com.

This book is available as an electronic download or more copies can be purchased (in printed format) at www.StrivingForImperfection.com. His first book, *The Shade of a Tree is the Very Best Shade There Is: 135 Lessons to Share with Your Children As They Grow Up* is available at www.ShadeOfATree.com

MEMBER
NSA
NATIONAL SPEAKERS ASSOCIATION

If you liked this book, you'll love...

Shade Of A Tree Is The Very Best Shade There Is... is for parents and children. It includes a FREE PDF version of the book for viewing electronically.

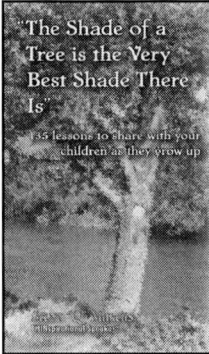

The book is a quick, light, heartwarming, read that you can do in an hour or so - but the lessons will stay with you for years

Hundreds of copies of this book have been sold to foster parents and teachers. A teacher in Houston, Texas even starts each day by putting a lesson on the board and having the class discuss it! Many times, after reading the book, people buy additional copies for gifts and for other family members.

A FREE e-book is included with every printed book purchase.

**Order the CD and
get the e-Book download FREE!**

Serenity in Parenting Audio

Serenity in Parenting is not just about parenting. it's about giving to yourself when everyone else is trying to take away.

This one-hour uplifting presentation delivered at a foster parent conference will inspire, guide, motivate - and provide great advice. You don't need to be a parent to pick up tips. learn goal setting techniquest, and feel better about life after listening to this presentation.

A FREE audio download (mp3) is included with every purchase when ordered on line.

To order, call toll free
866.762.7287 or visit
www.InspirationForParents.com

CD $15 + $4.50 shipping
CASSETTE $10 + $4.50 shipping
MP3 $4.95 + no shipping

**Order the CD or cassette and get the
MP3 download FREE!**

Save Money - Order the CD and
***The Shade of a Tree* together**
**at www.ShadeOfATree.com and get a reduced
rate of only $24.95 + $1 shipping!**

7 Lessons of Prosperity

Can one actually find
pleasure in taxes? Probably
not. But, after hearing
this delightful story, you
will be more prosperous
and appreciate what you have.
(You'll also never look at a towel rack the same
way!)

Prosperity is not about how much you own, it's
about how you feel. Increase your prosperity the
moment you listen to this CD or MP3.

**A FREE audio download (mp3) is included
with every purchase when ordered on line.**

Contact Information:

Scott "Q" Marcus
2521 E Street
Eureka, CA 95501
707.442.6243 • 866.SMARCUS
scottq@scottqmarcus.com

Scott's Websites:

www.scottqmarcus.com
www.THINspiration.com
www.CruiseTheBetterLife.com
www.TheEatingCycle.com
www.ShadeOfATree.com
www.InspirationForParents.com
www.FosterParentInspiration.com
www.StrivingForImperfection.com
www.7LessonsOfProsperity.com
www.NoBlackAndWhiteThinking

Make sure to sign up for Scott's FREE
motivational e-zine at any of the above
websites. You will not be spammed and you can
unsubscribe any time you wish.

Blogs:

www.tsblogs.com/imperfection
http://scottq.blogspot.com